the Treasure Hunters

By Dr. Scott
Turansky and
Joanne Miller
RN, BSN

8 Session
Children's
Program
Discovering
God's
Treasures in
Family Life
– for Children
Ages 3-12

Authors
Dr. Scott Turansky and
Joanne Miller, RN, BSN

Graphic Designer
Ellen Cranstoun

Creative Development Team
Candy Fithian
Aletheia Schmidt

Unless otherwise noted, Scripture quotations are from the Holy Bible, NEW INTERNATIONAL VERSION. Copyright ©1978 by the New York International Bible Society. Used by permission of Zondervan Bible Publishers.

Published in Lawrenceville, NJ by Effective Parenting, Inc.

Effective Parenting is a nonprofit corporation committed to the communication of sound biblical parenting principles through teaching, counseling, and the publication of written, audio, and video materials.

Printed in the USA
First Printing, January 2006

For information regarding permission or to find other resources for the family, contact:

 NATIONAL CENTER for BIBLICAL Parenting

76 Hopatcong Drive, Lawrenceville, NJ 08648-4136
(800) 771-8334 or (609) 771-8002
Email: parent@biblicalparenting.org
Web: biblicalparenting.org

Dear Teacher,

Children need a vision for being successful in family life. Changing behavior is important and this curriculum is full of helpful suggestions. But real change takes place in the heart. As children make adjustments on a deeper level, those changes will last forever. Through this curriculum children will learn how to follow instructions, deal with bad attitudes, accept no as an answer and other helpful relational skills, but it's our desire that the teaching in these areas will lead to significant heart change. You, as a teacher, have the opportunity to help kids learn more about the treasures of family life. Take time to talk to kids about why all this is important. The solutions to life are heart-based solutions.

Blessings,

Scott Turansky   *Joanne Miller*

the Treasure Hunters

How to Use This Curriculum

Teacher Note: You are the leader of a treasure hunt. Hidden within the common routines of family life are the treasures children need to be successful in their lives. God designed it that way. Your job is to help children see the treasure and understand its value.

Many kids don't realize why common tasks such as following instructions, receiving correction, and accepting no as an answer are important. They often see these directions and limitations as interruptions in their lives. Nothing could be further from the truth. God placed children in families for a reason. If they can discover the treasure now, they'll grow up with skills, maturity, and character that will benefit them forever.

Of course, communicating these things is a challenge for any parent or teacher. This curriculum is designed to communicate truths in fun and creative ways. Your excitement and enthusiasm about God's Word and God's success principles are important as you help your students discover some of the greatest treasures of their lives.

Parent Note: This material is also designed for family use, giving you meaningful family activities. Have fun with the concepts here and weave the ideas into your daily interaction with your children. When kids grasp a vision for seeing the treasure, great things happen.

So many activities are offered in this curriculum that you could do one or two at a time and have months of fun learning these concepts. Don't rush it. The goal isn't to get through the material. It's to get the concepts into your children's hearts.

Length of Lesson: Each session is designed to provide an hour to an hour and a half of fun and learning. However, the material can be shortened or lengthened depending on your needs. A family might choose to teach each lesson over four or five evenings. A Parenting Seminar Outreach children's program may last an hour and a half. The material was written with these options in mind. Most people find that this curriculum offers more material than can be used in the time allotted. Choose the parts you want to emphasize. Don't feel you have to do it all.

Other Resources: Although this children's curriculum can stand alone, it was written to complement the parent training video series entitled *Parenting is Heart Work.* Eight sessions on DVD and a Leader's Guide with reproducible participant guide are available for use in churches, small groups, and individual families. Learn more at www.biblicalparenting.org.

Order of Activities: Each lesson is divided into parts and is designed with children's developmental needs in mind. But children are all different and you may find it helpful to rearrange the lesson based on the needs of your students. As with all curriculum it's important to remember that you are not teaching material, you are teaching children. For example, you may choose to move the snack or the game to an earlier time because you sense the need for a change of pace during the session. So know your lesson well enough to use it as a tool to give your students a vision for finding God's treasures and enhancing family life.

the Treasure Hunters

Plan Ahead: Each lesson has games, activities, and crafts. Some require shopping, cutting, photocopying, or saving supplies. Take a few minutes now and highlight the supplies needed for each lesson. Make a shopping list or find helpers to prepare the craft projects in advance. Working ahead may even allow you to add that little extra touch to make the craft special.

It's best to create a model of the craft before you get to class to avoid surprises at the last minute. Also take time to do the science activities in advance to make sure they work for you.

Parent Letters: At the end of each lesson is a parent letter that explains to the parent what the child has learned in that session and gives suggestions for continuing the training at home. The first letter (on the next page) can be given out in advance or at the beginning of Session 1. Each subsequent letter may be sent home with the children at the end of that lesson.

The parent letters contained in this curriculum are from the National Center for Biblical Parenting. Please feel free to put them on your own letterhead and make them from you. If you'd like electronic versions of these letters in an RTF format so that you don't have to retype them you may download the file at: www.biblicalparenting.org/treasurehunters.html.

The Lesson Theme: Every lesson has a theme. That theme is described in one or two sentences and can be repeated over and over again by the teacher during transitions and activities. The goal is to repeat the theme about 10-15 times so that when children go home and Mom or Dad asks what they learned, they will tell their parents the theme.

Snack Ideas: A special snack idea that ties into the lesson is included in each session. Recipes are provided to make homemade treats but you can also feel free to purchase similar snacks if you prefer.

Parenting is Heart Work

The authors of the *Treasure Hunters* have also written the parent training book entitled, *Parenting is Heart Work.* In fact, that book provides the foundation for these lessons. It's not required but should you choose to read it, suggestions of where to read along are provided with each lesson. You may obtain the book at www.biblicalparenting.org

76 Hopatcong Drive, Lawrenceville, NJ 08648-4136
(800) 771-8334 or (609) 771-8002
Email: parent@biblicalparenting.org
Web: biblicalparenting.org

Some Things Your Child Will Be Learning

Dear Parent,

Over the next several weeks your child will learn how to be more effective in your family. Using Bible stories, crafts, activities, and games, we'll teach children how to do better at following instructions, receiving correction, accepting a no answer, and having a good attitude.

We understand that parenting challenges in family life are frustrating. Most parents get angry with their kids, some more frequently than others. We've all heard the suggestions that we need to count to ten and develop more patience. Unfortunately those kinds of solutions don't address the real problem – our kids are doing the wrong thing. We need a strategy that goes deeper and addresses the heart.

The heart is the place where kids develop conclusions about life. It contains emotions, desires, convictions, and beliefs. If we only focus on behavior then children may change for a short time but the real lasting change is illusive.

That's why we've developed this particular curriculum. We know that children need to learn more effective ways to relate in family life. We've chosen eight areas where kids often have struggles. Each session covers one of those areas. A letter like this one will come home with your child each week telling you what we emphasized on that day. Here's how you can make the most of this program.

First, pray for and with your child. Pray that God will make your family strong. Tell your child that you are learning to be a better parent and that's not easy at times. But if we all grow then our family will have greater strength and closeness.

Secondly, talk about the things your child is learning through this program. Each letter will tell you about the theme for that lesson. We're trying to reinforce the very things you're teaching at home. We hope and pray that the interactions in the class will provide you with teaching points at home.

Thirdly, practice. Look for ways to emphasize the truth in real life. New patterns take time to develop. Work on new routines to replace old ones. Remember that parenting is hard work because parenting is *heart* work. These truths will help you reach the hearts of your children.

Blessings,

Scott Turansky   Joanne Miller
National Center for Biblical Parenting
www.biblicalparenting.org

the Treasure Hunters

Contents

The Treasure Hidden in Following Instructions

Preparing Your Heart to Teach Session 1

How good are you, as an adult, at following instructions? In the midst of the daily routines of life, we all must comply with others' guidelines. Some people do better at it than others. God uses authorities in our lives to guide and direct us every day. One of the reasons it's so important to learn to follow others is that it prepares us to follow God. Even those who are strong leaders must learn how to follow someone else.

God speaks often to his children. Sometimes that speaking comes directly through his Word. Other times it happens in our hearts or through someone else. Those who are accustomed to following instructions are more readily able to hear from God when he speaks to them. Those who are resistant to instructions often find listening to God more difficult.

Take a moment and ask yourself how you're doing in this area. It's hard to teach children to do something that we ourselves struggle with. Thank God for the people in your life who help train you in this area. Thank them as well and commit to listening more attentively to the instructions of others and to God.

What Children Learn in Session 1

Hidden within obedience are the secret ingredients children need to be successful in life. God knows that, and that's one of the reasons why he placed children in families. Kids must learn now how to be successful as employees, team members and future mates. When kids learn to obey, they learn all kinds of helpful things that will equip them for later in life.

A good Instruction Routine contains several components. Parents often expect obedience but kids don't recognize its value so they resist. This session gives children a vision for the benefits of learning to follow instructions well.

Theme: Following instructions means I come when called, give a response, and report back.

Repeat these words over and over again so that kids can give an answer to the following question: What did you learn? Answer: Following instructions means I come when called, give a response, and report back. If you practice that question and answer, and emphasize this truth, then parents will hear these words at home when they ask their kids what they learned. Remind kids that responsiveness to instructions is a treasure inside of you that people will love.

Read Along in the Book, "Parenting is Heart Work"

The Introduction to **Parenting is Heart Work** provides motivation to look past behavior to the heart. It's easy to focus only on behavior because that's what's visible. But the heart is more complicated. Teaching children to follow instructions has some definite heart implications. Chapter 4 shows how working on behavior the right way can actually contribute to heart change. Behavior is a symptom. In fact, sometimes working on behavior becomes a way to get to the heart. The two are linked closely together. In order to gain the most from an Instruction Routine it's necessary to keep an eye on the heart. Character qualities like cooperation and responsibility grow out of a good Instruction Routine.

Session 1

Theme

Following instructions means
I come when called, give a response,
and report back.

Welcome Activity

Preparation:

Photocopy onto cardstock the name tags at the end of this lesson. Punch holes and cut yarn into 16″ lengths. Provide crayons or markers.

"Love the Lord your God. Listen to his voice."
Deuteronomy 30:20

What children first experience when they walk into the room is important. Consider things like music, decorations, and a friendly greeting. Welcome kids by saying things like, "Oh here's another Treasure Hunter to join our group." Have children sit down at a table and color a Treasure Hunter name tag. Help the children with the yarn so they can wear their name tags after they are decorated.

Together Time

Use the ideas below along with your own thoughts and the Bible to dialogue with the children and help them see that hidden within obedience are the secret ingredients that make a person successful in life.

Object Lesson
Can You Obey?

In just a moment we're going to play a game. I'm going to have you all laugh but when I put my hand in the air, I want you to stop laughing and get ready to hear what I say next. I want to see who will obey and stop. Okay, ready? Laugh. Allow that to go on for about 5 seconds and then

put your hand in the air. It's helpful to have a couple of other leaders participate with you because sometimes children don't respond quickly to this game and they continue on. That, by the way, is a good reason to play it and to teach this lesson. "Many of you obeyed and stopped right away, but some didn't. I want to see if you can obey. Let's try again." Laugh.

You can play this game a few times replacing "laugh" with "grumble," or "whisper."

Children have various responses to this game. Some will rebel and not stop, but most of the time kids will get into the activity and follow instructions. Some will even freeze in place.

Tell the kids that you like the way they are obeying and that obeying is an important part of life. In this lesson we're going to talk about obeying and some practical ways that kids can do their part to follow instructions well. Most importantly, there's an attitude in the heart that leads to cooperation and that's a treasure.

Bible Story
God is Looking for Kids Who Will Listen

Samuel didn't live with his parents. He was raised by another family. The dad in this new family was Eli. He was a priest and his job was to take care of God's house. Samuel learned how to sweep and clean and run errands for Eli the priest. He learned how to carry firewood, and straighten things up in the house of the Lord.

Samuel wanted to do what was right. Two other boys in this new family did the wrong thing. They were always getting into trouble. They were mean and would fight with people. But Samuel loved God and wanted to do what was right. Eli could see that something was different about this little boy. Samuel wasn't like his own sons. His heart was in the right place.

One night Samuel went to bed just like any other night. He lay down on his mat on the floor and fell asleep. Sometime later he heard something that woke him up. Someone was calling his name.

"Samuel, Samuel."

Photocopied by permission from the National Center for Biblical Parenting

It must be Eli. I wonder what he wants. Samuel got up and ran into Eli's room. "Yes, Eli, here I am. What do you want?"

Kids, when someone calls you, do you come over to that person to talk to them? That's the kind thing to do. Some kids just yell back to the other room, "Yeah, whadaya want?" That isn't kind. The best thing to do is what Samuel did. He heard someone call his name and he went to find out why.

If you want to be successful in life then you'll want to learn to follow instructions well at home. In fact, God has hidden a treasure within obedience. What if I told you there was a golden treasure hidden in a cave but you'd have to dig and work hard to get it? Would you do the work? Sure you would because you want all that gold. You want to be successful in life and God wants you to be successful too. That's why he's given you a treasure but he's hidden it in a place where you have to work hard. God has hidden a treasure inside following instructions.

If you learn how to follow instructions well, you'll gain a great treasure. Let's talk about three things that you can do when you're given an instruction. First, come when called. Second, give a response like "Okay Mom." And third, report back when you get the job done. What are those three things? (Repeat them a couple of times so kids get the idea.)

Samuel knew how to follow instructions. That's why he went right into Eli's room when he heard his name called. If you do that same thing, Mom and Dad will say to themselves, "Wow, this child is very responsible."

But it wasn't Eli who called him. "I didn't call you. Go back to bed." So Samuel returned to his cot and lay down quietly.

"Samuel, Samuel." *There it is again. Eli must have changed his mind and now he wants something.* So again Samuel got up and went into the other room and he said, "Yes Eli, what can I do for you?"

When you're involved in a project or you're tired, it's not easy to come when someone calls you, is it? Some kids ignore their parents when they call, but not Samuel. He wanted to do what was right. He got up again and went into Eli's room.

"I didn't call you," said Eli. Samuel was puzzled. Someone was calling him, but he didn't know who it was. So, he went back to bed.

It happened one more time and Eli said to Samuel. "This time when you go back to bed, if you hear someone calling you, then say, 'Speak Lord, for your servant is listening.' It sounds like God wants to talk to you, Samuel."

And that's what Samuel did. He went back to bed and listened. After a short time he heard the voice again. "Samuel, Samuel."

"Speak Lord, for your servant is listening." At that moment God spoke to Samuel. This was the first time but not the last. Samuel was a young boy who wanted to serve the Lord and listen to him, and God wanted to talk to Samuel.

Kids, one of the reasons God wants you to learn to come when you're called and listen to your parents is so that you'll be ready. Lots of practice listening to parents gets you ready to listen to God. He wants to speak to you. Sometimes he'll speak to you through his Word, the Bible. Other times he'll speak inside your heart, but will you be able to hear him? You will if you learn to obey Mom and Dad. Listening and obeying your parents is practice for listening to God. He is looking for kids who know how to obey because he wants to use them in this world to serve him.

This Bible story was taken from 1 Samuel 3.

Bible Verse

Deuteronomy 30:20
"Love the LORD your God, listen to his voice."

Session 1

Transition

What are the three things we talked about that you can do when you're given an instruction: Come when called, give a response, and report back. Good. I'm going to test you on those three things again in a few minutes but right now I'm going to see if you can follow instructions as we play a game together. You have to listen carefully now because this game requires that you follow instructions.

Game (For Older Children)
The Hand Game

The purpose of this game is to have fun but also to help children understand that following instructions is sometimes difficult and requires work to do the job well.

Children sit in groups of five around a table with all hands flat on the table palms down. Each person picks their right hand up and places it face down to the right of the left hand of the person on their right. Now each person should have two hands in front of them neither of which are their own. One player starts by lifting fingers only and hitting the table once. The next hand clockwise repeats by tapping once, and the next, and the next, and so on. Any hand can tap once or twice. Two taps reverses the direction. If someone moves a hand out of turn, that hand is removed from the table. The game continues until only two hands remain.

As children get into this game they begin to give each other instructions, again providing more opportunity to discuss the value of listening to instructions.

Use this game to talk about always being ready to receive instructions. You never know how things might change and so you always have to be ready. The same is true in family life. If you are always ready to receive instructions, then when Mom or Dad asks you to do something you can stop what you're doing and respond right away.

Following instructions is the sign of a good employee too. So, if you work hard to learn this when you're young, you'll be growing a treasure in your heart that others will see as you get older. People will say, "Wow. She is a great helper. I want her on my team." Or, "I like the way he responds the first time. I'm going to hire him to work for me."

Game (For Younger Children)
The Hand Game

Have everyone put their hands on the table. "See if you can follow instructions now. Put one hand on top of your other hand. Good. Put them back on the table again. Now put one hand on top of your neighbor's hand next to you. Good. Now put both hands in your lap. Put one hand on your head. Put one hand on the table. Wiggle your fingers in the air. I'm seeing if you can follow instructions." Some younger children may be able to tap around the table one person at a time. Remember that the goal is learning to follow instructions even when it's difficult.

Explain to children that they always need to be ready to receive an instruction. The same is true in family life and following instructions is a treasure.

Transition

Now I'm going to ask you a very important question: What three things can you remember about receiving instructions? Come when called, give a response, report back. Good. I'm going to see if you can remember those three things after we're done making a craft and then playing a game.

Craft
The Chicken Game

Preparation: Photocopy the "Chicken" page at the end of this lesson onto card stock. You'll need a paper plate for each child, one brad for each child, crayons or markers, and scissors.

This activity serves as a craft and then as a fun game for following directions.

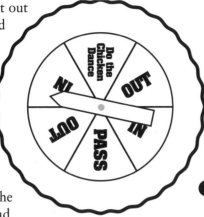

First, have children cut out the "spinner" base and glue it onto the back of a paper plate. Use a ballpoint pen to poke a hole in the center of the spinner base and a hole puncher to make a hole in the pointer. Use a brad to attach the pointer to the spinner. Fasten the brad loosely so the pointer can spin freely.

Have the children color the six eggs and then cut them out.

Playing the Game: Start by doing the Chicken Dance. This is a fun, high energy, dance that lasts about 2-3 seconds. Have everyone do it together first. Stand up. Put your thumbs under your armpits, flap your elbows up and down like a chicken, bend at the waist, turn around two times, squawk like a chicken and then sit down. That is the chicken dance.

Some children may, at first find this rather embarrassing. That's okay. Kids seem to get into it more as the game progresses. If someone doesn't want to do the chicken dance tell them they can just say "balk balk." As the game continues, children tend to grow in their willingness to do the dance. Take a group picture of those willing to do the Chicken Dance.

Set half the games aside and allow two people to share one game. Each player receives three eggs. As you play this game, spin the spinner. If it lands on IN you put one egg under the spinner. Then it's the next person's turn. If the spinner lands on OUT then you have to take one egg out. If it lands on "Chicken Dance" then you have to stand up and do the chicken dance.

The game ends when the first child gets all the eggs in. A child is out and must watch when he or she has no more eggs to remove. Acknowledge the winner and those who do the Chicken Dance.

For Younger Children

You may want to do most of the cutting, gluing, and assembling, and allow children just to color the pieces.

Have each child play with their own spinner, with the teacher directing one child at a time. It's especially fun for the young children to watch one of their peers get up and do the chicken dance. The kids take turns spinning and following the instructions before the next child's turn.

● ● ● ● ●

Transition

When you know how to follow instructions you can learn to play fun games. Why else do people follow instructions? Do grownups have to follow instructions? What if they didn't listen to the policeman or their boss at work? Where else do we listen to instructions (church, library, etc.)?

What are the three things about receiving instructions that you're trying to remember? Come when called, give a response, report back. Good. We're going to practice that right now as we do a role play together.

Role Play

Preparation: Make up the instruction cards as suggested in this activity.

"I have some different instructions written on pieces of paper here. I need a person to be the mom who will give the instructions, and someone to receive them who can act as a child." Set up several role play situations where the child is acting like he's busy playing, watching TV, asleep, or otherwise busy. The mom can also be busy, angry, gentle, or intense. Have children role play several positive and negative responses to instructions. Practice the three things that make a good instruction.

- Come when called
- Give a response
- Report back

Session 1

For instructions you might use some of these ideas:
- Move the trash can over to the door.
- Bring me five chairs and line them up here.
- Please get me a glass of water.
- Take four pencils and form them into a square.
- Write your name on the board along with your favorite kind of food.

Talk to the children about a right way and a wrong way to respond to instructions. Emphasize with kids the value of responding well with an "Okay Dad" kind of response. Also encourage children to report back by saying "I'm done," or "I did it. Would you like to check my work?"

● ● ● ● ● ───────

Transition

You guys are doing great at following instructions. We're going to play another game now and see how well you can do at giving and receiving instructions. Some of you will be giving instructions and some will be receiving them. I'm going to be listening to those who are receiving instructions to see if they say "Okay."

Activity (For Older Children)
Human Knot Game

Have children form into groups of five. Children should grab hands with others in the group following these guidelines: You can't hold the hand of the person next to you. You can't hold two hands of the same person. Once the hands are all grabbed then the group must "untie" the human knot, by listening to each other's instructions.

This is a fun game to watch and to participate in so it might be helpful to allow one group to go at a time while others watch and coach them on. Following instructions when a number of people are trying to lead can be a challenge and provides some interesting debriefing discussions afterwards.

Play the game 2-3 times especially listening to how children give and receive instructions. Talk about the process by asking, "How did it go?" "Who was

giving instructions?" "What happened when you listened?" "What happened when you didn't listen?"

Activity (For Younger Children)
Follow the Leader

Preparation: Provide enough hand towels for each pair of children to share one.

Divide children into pairs. Give each pair one hand towel. Have the children hold opposite ends of the towel. Tell them this is an activity to see how well you can lead and follow. Put several chairs around the room to create obstacles. Ask the leaders to guide the followers through the maze. After about 30 seconds, ring a bell or flash the lights, signifying that it's time to reverse roles and the follower becomes the leader. Go back and forth several times practicing leading and following.

After you're done, ask children "Which did you like best: leading or following?" Have a discussion about the importance of following the leader, following instructions, and listening to Mom and Dad as they try to lead the family.

Activity (For Younger Children)
Traffic Cop

Preparation: Make a stop sign out of red paper or cardboard using the template and instructions at the end of this lesson.

Have one child sit in a chair and have a second child march around the chair. When the "traffic cop" holds up the stop sign in the air, the "traffic" must stop. If the child doesn't stop, he must sit down and another child gets to be the traffic. Tell the children, "We want to see how well you can follow instructions on a sign." After playing this game a few times you may try to add an additional child as part of the traffic. As the numbers increase for the traffic, children tend not to pay attention to the stop sign. You may tell children that when the stop sign goes up, you must stop. If you don't stop then you have to come over to the watching area.

Talk about signs in life that give instructions and why they're important. Stop lights protect cars from crashing. A fire alarm tells people to get out of a building and so on. The important thing is that children learn how to obey whether it's a sign or spoken words. Following instructions is important.

● ● ● ● ●

Transition

Let's see who remembers the three things about receiving instructions? Good. Come when called, give a response, and report back. Now we'll eat some fun food if we can follow instructions.

Snack

Preparation: Purchase the ingredients on the recipe card at the end of this lesson. Photocopy the recipe card for each child. Provide a zip-lock bag for each child.

> **Treasure Recipe**
>
> Follow instructions and put the following things in your plastic bag.
>
> - 10 Goldfish
> - 5 Brown M&Ms
> - 6 Small Pretzels
> - 10 Raisins
> - 3 Orange M&Ms
> - 4 Jelly Beans
> - 7 Chex Pieces
> - 4 Green M&Ms
> - 8 Mini marshmallows
>
> (What do you do with the extra M&M's? The teachers get to eat them.)

This activity emphasizes "reporting back" in the instruction process. You might put the ingredients on the table and have children report when they're ready to have their work checked before they eat the recipe. Or you may have stations around the room where children go and get the ingredients, put them into their bag and report back. You will need to give the instructions verbally to younger children and guide them through the procedure. As children have fun eating, talk about the importance of following instructions and why reporting back is important. When kids report back they then get to hear things like "You did a good job," "Great," "I like that," and so on. Reporting back is an important part of the job.

Review and Close

Bring the children together to help them process the day's activities. Talk about the lessons learned from the activities and the Bible story. Following instructions is important. What kind of instructions do parents give to their children? Sometimes children aren't very good at receiving instructions. They whine, or complain, or have bad attitudes.

But learning how to follow instructions in your family is so important because God is preparing a treasure right now in your heart. When you learn to follow instructions at home you will become a better friend and a helpful adult. People will appreciate you more and others will see that you are growing up and learning how to listen.

We learned today that it's important to come when called. Getting close before receiving or giving instructions is very important because it strengthens relationships. Parents will be pleased when you learn to come when called. It makes the whole process run much better.

It's also important to learn to give an answer back when someone gives you an instruction. Start practicing this at home and you'll see some good things happen. Again, not only will your parents be pleased, but when you give an answer to others you are becoming a treasure. Teachers say, "My, that person responds very well." You will begin to develop a good reputation for yourself. And that itself is a treasure.

Be sure to end the instruction time by reporting back. Come back and say to Dad or Mom, "I finished the job." When you do that, parents are impressed and you get to hear Mom or Dad say, "Thank you." Or "Great, you're free to go." Most importantly, when you do these things you're learning how to receive instructions elsewhere in life. Others will be impressed and you'll be moving well on your way to being successful in life. One of the treasures in family life is learning to follow instructions. I'm going to ask you one more time what the three things are that we've talked about that make up following instructions? Come when called, give a response, and report back.

Session 1

Welcome Activity Instructions:

Photocopy this page onto heavy paper or cardstock and use it according to the instructions in this lesson.

"Love the Lord your God. Listen to his voice."
Deuteronomy 30:20

"Love the Lord your God. Listen to his voice."
Deuteronomy 30:20

"Love the Lord your God. Listen to his voice."
Deuteronomy 30:20

"Love the Lord your God. Listen to his voice."
Deuteronomy 30:20

"Love the Lord your God. Listen to his voice."
Deuteronomy 30:20

The Chicken Game

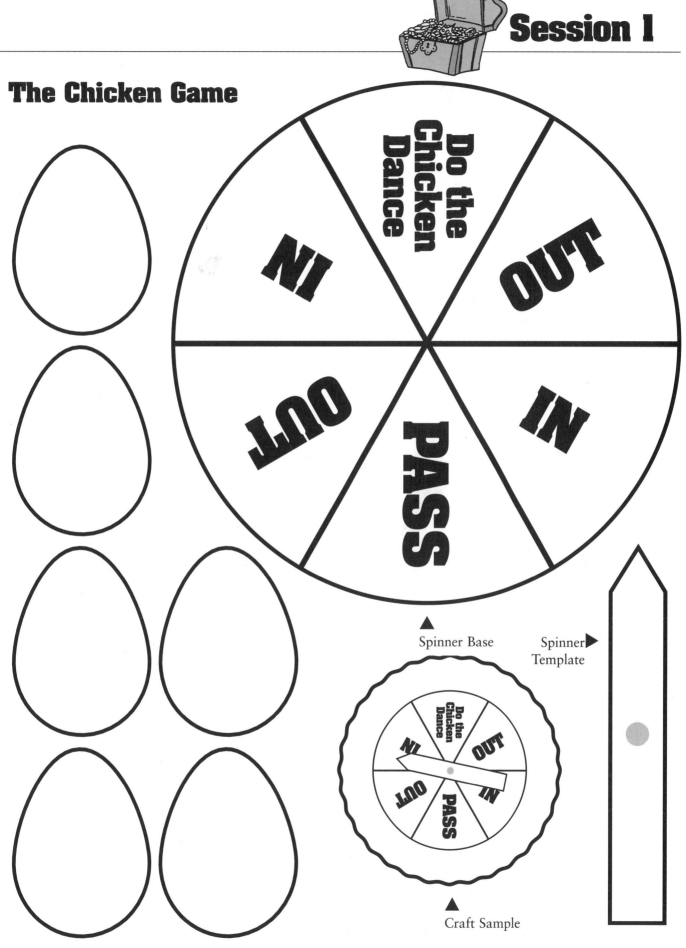

Spinner Base

Spinner Template

Craft Sample

Session 1

Traffic Cop Activity
Instructions:

Photocopy this page onto red construction paper. Cut out the sign and staple or tape it to a paint stir stick or other stick to use in the "Traffic Cop" Activity.

Snack

Treasure Recipe

Follow instructions and put the following things in your plastic bag.

- 10 Goldfish
- 5 Brown M&Ms
- 6 Small Pretzels
- 10 Raisins
- 3 Orange M&Ms
- 4 Jelly Beans
- 7 Chex Pieces
- 4 Green M&Ms
- 8 Mini marshmallows

(What do you do with the extra M&M's? The teachers get to eat them.)

Treasure Recipe

Follow instructions and put the following things in your plastic bag.

- 10 Goldfish
- 5 Brown M&Ms
- 6 Small Pretzels
- 10 Raisins
- 3 Orange M&Ms
- 4 Jelly Beans
- 7 Chex Pieces
- 4 Green M&Ms
- 8 Mini marshmallows

(What do you do with the extra M&M's? The teachers get to eat them.)

Treasure Recipe

Follow instructions and put the following things in your plastic bag.

- 10 Goldfish
- 5 Brown M&Ms
- 6 Small Pretzels
- 10 Raisins
- 3 Orange M&Ms
- 4 Jelly Beans
- 7 Chex Pieces
- 4 Green M&Ms
- 8 Mini marshmallows

(What do you do with the extra M&M's? The teachers get to eat them.)

Treasure Recipe

Follow instructions and put the following things in your plastic bag.

- 10 Goldfish
- 5 Brown M&Ms
- 6 Small Pretzels
- 10 Raisins
- 3 Orange M&Ms
- 4 Jelly Beans
- 7 Chex Pieces
- 4 Green M&Ms
- 8 Mini marshmallows

(What do you do with the extra M&M's? The teachers get to eat them.)

76 Hopatcong Drive, Lawrenceville, NJ 08648-4136
(800) 771-8334 or (609) 771-8002
Email: parent@biblicalparenting.org
Web: biblicalparenting.org

Teaching Children How to Follow Instructions

Dear Parent,

Giving instructions to children can be a challenge, especially when kids don't cooperate. In our lesson this week we talked about the benefit of following instructions and we taught the children three key elements that will make them successful in this area.

Theme: Following instructions means I come when called, give a response, and report back.

In order for children to change, though, parents must also change. We would suggest that a good Instruction Routine requires that parents connect with their kids by getting close to them before giving the instruction. Often this means calling children and teaching them to **come when called.**

After you give an instruction it's good for kids to respond with "Okay, Mom," or "Okay, Dad." **This response** is a common courtesy but it confirms that cooperation is developing.

Having children **report back** after they do the job gives you a chance to inspect their work, teach about thoroughness if necessary and then praise them. Take time to end every instruction time with affirmation. Release children after they've done the job. Kids need to know that they are done and they've accomplished what you've asked.

We used the Bible story about Samuel listening to God's voice and Deuteronomy 30:20 to teach children that learning to listen to God starts by obeying parents. We used other games and activities to emphasize this truth. You might ask your child about the Chicken Game and play it together. Be sure to follow instructions!

Blessings,

Scott Turansky   Joanne Miller
National Center for Biblical Parenting
www.biblicalparenting.org

Beliefs Feed Behavior

Preparing Your Heart to Teach Session 2

What you believe about life effects how you live. That's one of the reasons regular time with the Lord is so helpful. It has the ability to remind us of the most important things in life like inner peace with God instead of angry responses with others, or relationships with people instead of completing a to-do list, or trusting in God instead of getting upset with anxiety.

We all need frequent reminders to follow the Lord, listen to his voice, and choose what's most important. God continually does a work in our hearts as he transforms what we believe.

Take kindness for example. The small acts of kindness we give to others everyday say more about us than they do about the other person. A kind person is strong inside and reveals character that the mean person lacks. Holding a door for someone else to go first reveals unselfishness. Responding to an irritation with grace instead of anger demonstrates self-control and humility. Putting up with someone who is annoying shows patience.

As you help children evaluate the difference between meanness and kindness in this lesson, take time to evaluate your own heart and ways you might continue to develop some inner strength as well.

What Children Learn in Session 2

Children often believe strange things and those beliefs then effect how they live and act. Parents often look for ways to address behavior in children but if the beliefs themselves aren't addressed then change is only temporary. In this lesson children will be challenged to think about kindness and meanness in a different way. Kind people are strong on the inside and mean people are weak. That truth is reinforced over and over again through the game, activities, craft, and Bible story. Saul of Tarsus was a bully who God transformed and God used the kind man, Ananias, to help in the process.

Theme: Kind people are strong on the inside.

As you repeat these words throughout the lesson you will contribute to a healthy belief system in your students. The children will go home thinking about these words and will be able to share them when Mom or Dad asks, "What did you learn today?"

Read Along in the Book, "Parenting is Heart Work"

Chapter 9 introduces the biblical concept of talking to oneself in the heart, referencing several Bible stories and scriptures passages that give greater understanding. Some children are internal processors and it can be difficult to know what's going on in their hearts. Other kids are external processors. They say everything that's going on inside and they act out to solve their problems. Both kinds of children are wrestling with heart issues. Chapter 11 elaborates on meditation and how to help children develop healthy thought patterns. Meditation is usually considered a spiritual discipline, and certainly it is. But people also meditate on anger, fear, worry and all kinds of unproductive things. Four suggestions are given in this chapter to help children change how they meditate.

Session 2

Theme

Kind people are strong on the inside.

Welcome Activity

As children enter the room have them sit at the table and make binoculars (younger children) or funny glasses (older children). Young children love the binoculars and this craft will tie in well with the Treasure Hunter theme and the story of Saul becoming blind. Older children can take time to decorate and enjoy making the glasses and then showing others their creativity.

Talk to children about how people can see things differently in life. When hearts see things differently it has to do with what people believe.

Binoculars (For Younger Children)

Preparation:
Photocopy onto construction paper or cardstock the template at the end of this lesson. Also have markers or crayons, a hole punch, yarn, plastic wrap, rubber bands, glue, masking tape, and two toilet paper tubes ready for each child.

Have children decorate the covering for the binoculars using markers or crayons. Use masking tape to fasten two tubes together. Use rubber bands to hold plastic wrap on one end of the tubes. Punch holes in the outside of the tubes and put yarn through the holes to make a strap to wear around the neck. Wrap the cover around the binoculars and glue in place.

Funny Glasses (For Older Children)

Preparation: Cut one toilet paper tube in half to make two tubes to be used as lenses for the glasses. Also have markers or crayons, a hole punch, rubber bands, string or chenille wire, plastic wrap, and construction paper ready for each child.

Tape plastic wrap on the one end of each tube. Using a hole punch, fasten the two lenses together by tying a string or using chenille wire to create a nose bridge, holding the lenses about 1/2 inch apart. On the outside parts of the lenses punch holes and tie a rubber band through the hole to go around the head. You can either use a large rubber band or several small rubber bands fastened together. Decorate the glasses with pieces of construction paper. Have children wear their glasses and show their creativity.

Use the binoculars or funny glasses to talk about going on a Treasure Hunt or seeing treasure that others can't see. We're going to learn about some valuable treasure in our lesson today. You might also describe how glasses help us see more clearly. These special glasses or binoculars remind us that we need to see life differently than others do sometime. Be sure to take a group picture of the kids with their funny glasses and binoculars.

● ● ● ● ●

Together Time

Use the ideas below along with your own thoughts and the Bible to dialogue with the children and help them see that what you believe about life makes all the difference in how you treat other people.

Object Lesson
How Strong is Paper?

Preparation: You'll need three 8 oz paper or plastic cups, two pieces of 8 1/2″ x 11″ paper and some water.

Put two cups face up on a table about 6″ apart. Fill the third cup with water. Take one of the pieces of paper and write the word "MEAN" in big letters. Ask children, "Do you think this piece of paper is strong enough to hold this cup of water balanced between these two cups?" Place the piece of paper across the two cups and it will sag in the middle on its own. "No, this piece of paper is

weak. It reminds me of some people who act tough and bully other people. They aren't kind but they're mean instead."

Today we're going to talk about people who are strong on the inside. Some people pretend to be strong and they think that if they are mean then that proves that they are strong. They are really weak on the inside.

I want to show you how this piece of paper can hold up this cup of water. We're going to write "kind" on this piece of paper. Now what are some kind things you might do in your home?" As children mention acts of kindness, hold the paper horizontally and fold it like a fan with 1/2 inch between each fold. Write some of those acts of kindness on the folds. Each fold represents an act of kindness. When you're done you'll have a fan-folded piece of paper that is 11 inches long. "Now let's see if this piece of paper can hold up this cup of water." Place the folded piece of paper on the cups resting on several points of the fan and place the cup on the paper. It holds the water.

"I want you to remember a very important truth today: Kind people are strong on the inside. Mean people are weak on the inside."

Bible Story
A Bully Learns a Lesson

Can you think of any bullies in the Bible? Goliath, Cain, King Saul, Haman are just a few. Today, I want to tell you about a bully in the Bible. His name was Saul of Tarsus. Saul mistreated Christians. He didn't like them. He would travel from one place to another and he would hurt them. Many people had to run away and move to another city because Saul was so mean. But that didn't even stop Saul. He went after people in other cities, trying to hurt them.

Do you think people liked Saul? No, they didn't. When they heard that Saul

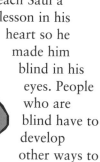

was coming, they would hide. Saul was mean to people because he was weak on the inside. Maybe you know someone who is mean. They say unkind things, hurt other people, and take things that don't belong to them. They're just weak on the inside. Saul was like that.

One day Saul was on a trip up to Damascus to find more Christians to be mean to. On his way, a terrible thing happened to him. A very large light flashed all around him and it blinded him. He couldn't see. He fell to the ground and then he heard a voice say, "Saul, Saul, why do you persecute me?"

Saul was shocked. *Who was this person speaking?* He didn't know so he asked, "Who are you?"

"I am Jesus whom you are persecuting. Get up and go into the city and you will be told what to do."

Saul looked up but he couldn't see a thing. He was blind. Everyone close your eyes for a moment. Imagine what kind of things you wouldn't be able to see. You couldn't watch TV. You couldn't enjoy a pretty sunset or look at nice flowers. If you were blind you would have a hard time walking around. You can open your eyes now. If you were blind, what would you miss the most? (Allow children to answer that question.)

Saul had a problem. He was mean. Because he was mean, he had a heart problem. In fact, in his heart he was blind to other people's feelings. He didn't care how bad he made other people feel with his hurtful actions. He didn't see how he was hurting others. People who are mean are blind on the inside.

God wanted to teach Saul a lesson in his heart so he made him blind in his eyes. People who are blind have to develop other ways to get around, experience life, and solve problems. People who are blind are often stronger on the inside because of their blindness.

Mean people are weak on the inside. God wanted to teach Saul an important lesson so that he would become strong on the inside. So God blinded him with the flash of light. While Saul was blind, God said, "I am going to use you as my servant. I want you to help other people who are blind on the inside see more clearly." His friends led him into the city of Damascus to wait and see what to do next. For three days Saul was blind. That would be hard. It would be hard to eat, hard to talk to people, hard to take a walk. Three days is a long time to be blind.

Now, there was a man who lived in the city of Damascus named Ananias. God came to him in a vision and said, "I have a job for you. There's a man who needs to be healed of blindness and I want you to be the one to visit him and help him. His name is Saul of Tarsus."

Ananias was shocked. "Lord, I've heard about Saul. He's the one who's been so mean to the Christians and the reason he's here is to be mean some more."

God said, "Ananias, I want you to go anyway. I want you to show kindness to Saul because I have a special plan for him."

How do you think Ananias felt when God told him to go and be kind to the mean bully? That would be hard. I think God chose Ananias because he knew that he could even be kind to a bully. Not too many people could do that, but Ananias was strong on the inside. He was ready. He went to Saul, the bully, and talked to him kindly. The Bible tells us that he placed his hands on Saul. That would be difficult for me. I would have a hard time touching a bully. But Ananias was strong on the inside and he knew that God wanted Saul to be strong on the inside too. God knew that Saul was ready to have Jesus living in his heart.

Saul was a changed man. No longer was he a bully. When God changed Saul, he gave him an inner strength that made him a kind man, eager to help others and ready to care for those who were

hurting. God changed Saul's heart in a lot of ways, but one of the things he did was turn Saul from being mean to being kind.

God wants to change your heart too. When you have Jesus living inside your heart, he develops inner strength. One of those inner strengths is kindness. It takes a strong person on the inside to be kind to others, because kindness takes work. It's hard to be kind sometimes, helping others, letting others go first, doing things someone else's way. Kindness takes work but it reveals an inner strength we all want to have.

This Bible story was taken from Acts 9:1-19.

Bible Verse

Philippians 4:13
"I can do everything through him who gives me strength."

● ● ● ● ● ──────────────

Transition
We talked in our story about two kinds of strength. What shows that you are strong on the inside? Yes, the ability to be kind. Now we want to play a game to talk about strength.

Game
Tug of War

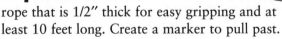

Preparation: Obtain a rope that is 1/2" thick for easy gripping and at least 10 feet long. Create a marker to pull past.

Have children sit down on the floor to watch this event. Ask for volunteers to try the tug of war. Have two children on each side grab the rope and pull. The winners pull the other team across a line on the floor or a marker like a chair. After each turn, ask children for some kind things they can say about those who won and those who lost. Affirm children who give kind comments by saying, "I can tell you're strong on the inside by your kind words." Or "That was a kind comment, a sign that you have inner strength." Remember

that the real benefit of this game is not that the winner is the one who can pull the strongest, but the ones who are able to demonstrate kindness the best.

Tug of Kindness

Now choose only two people to sit on the floor opposite each other as if they were going to have a Tug of War. This is different. It's a Tug of Kindness. The participants must keep their two feet and two knees together and in front of them. Using the rope, and pulling together, have the children try to stand up. The goal is for both children to work together so that they are both standing.

For Younger Children

Younger children may not grasp the full idea of a tug of war but they like to pull on it. So you might have two or three children take one side of the rope, and you, the teacher, take the other and ask the kids to pull. "Show me your muscles and how strong you are." Talk about the difference between strong muscles and a strong heart of kindness. When you do the Tug of Kindness, first have the teacher try to pull one or more children up, and then have children help pull the teacher up. We're working together on teamwork in this exercise.

● ● ● ● ●

Transition

Kindness takes work doesn't it? You have to think a little more in order to say something kind. Sometimes I want to say something kind but I'm not sure what to say. That means that I need more practice at thinking of nice comments. Kindness is like a muscle. If you exercise it, it becomes stronger. Think about ways that you can say kind things today as we continue to work together.

Craft
Stone Paperweight

KIND

Preparation: Obtain several smooth stones. The size of the stones may vary, but usually stones that are about 4″ in diameter

work best. You can usually obtain them inexpensively at a local garden shop if you don't have access to stones in your area. You'll also need felt, glue, a fat permanent marker, and other supplies to use for decorating.

Children can put felt on the bottom of the stone and then decorate the top with glitter, sequins, or yarn. Put the word KIND on the stone with glue and glitter, paint, or even a fat permanent marker. Have children decorate the stone around the edges. Older children can use yarn to make hair or a funny face. Talk about how people can be hard (mean) or soft (kind) to others. This craft is a reminder that kind people are strong on the inside.

For Younger Children

Younger children often find painting the rocks easier. Provide paint and brushes for kids and let them decorate their rock. Glue the felt on the bottom so they can use it as a paperweight. If it's not dry by the time class is over, children can take home the rock on a paper towel.

● ● ● ● ●

Transition

Most people think that meanness is a sign of strength. Bullies boss people around and look for ways to hurt others. They sometimes think that being mean is funny and they laugh about it. That's even more hurtful. Kindness is a different way to think. It means that we look at people differently. Instead of making fun of someone just to get a laugh, it's better to think about how other people feel. This next activity is fun because it helps us see that sometimes we're just not thinking the right way.

Activity (For Older Children)
Optical Illusions

Preparation:
Photocopy one teaching copy of the optical illusions at the end of this lesson.

Show the children the illusions and ask them

questions like "Which is longer?" or "Which is bigger?" Then have the children measure to see which is actually longer or bigger. The fun is in discovering that what you think you see isn't quite right. Use this activity to help children understand that mean may seem strong but it really isn't. Kind people are strong on the inside. Mean people are weak on the inside.

Activity (For Younger Children)
Kindness Color Sheet

Photocopy the "Kind people are strong on the inside" poster at the end of this lesson. Have kids color it as you reinforce the theme. Although these children usually can't read, they can take the sheet home for parents to review the lesson.

Transition

People can be mean in all kinds of different ways. We're going to do an activity I think you're going to enjoy. Move the chairs and tables out of the way for this activity and have children sit in a large circle on the floor. Meanness is weakness on the inside. Kindness is strength on the inside.

Activity
A Discussion About Meanness

Preparation: You'll need a lot of newspaper for this activity.

Give children stacks of newspaper and have them wad up pieces into crumpled paper balls. Then ask for a volunteer to be the victim. "Who would like to be my victim? The victim will get paper thrown at him." It's not usually too hard to find a victim. Give the victim some instructions. "Imagine that these people are throwing real rocks and that each

one hurts you. Your job is to act out the pain of the rocks hitting you." Have children gather round, you say "go" and let the paper balls fly.

Then have everyone sit down and ask the following questions. Allow several students to give answers.

"How do you think our victim felt getting rocks thrown at him?"
"How do you think he would have felt if they were real rocks?"
"Sometimes people throw rocks when they're mean but what are some other ways that people are mean?"

There is an American proverb that says, "Sticks and stones may break my bones but words can never hurt me." Do you think that's true? Guide the discussion in ways that allow children to see that their words can cause more damage than they realize because they hurt a person's feelings. You may want to have fun throwing the paper at another victim, at each other, or at the teacher. Be sure to explain that this game isn't really mean because the people involved agree to do it. There aren't really any victims here because we're just playing the game in fun. Then have fun. Make sure the last part of the game has children throwing all the paper into a plastic trash bag to clean up.

Transition

What you feed your heart determines what comes out. An old Indian story talks about a black dog and a white dog that live inside of each person. The black dog is mean, unkind, negative, violent, and hurtful. The white dog is kind, considerate, unselfish, and generous. Which dog is going to win? The answer is: the one you feed the most. If you spend time thinking about unkind things then you play out meanness in your heart over and over again. If you think about kindness then kind things will come out. Jesus said something very similar. He said that out of the heart the mouth speaks. If we want to have kind words and actions, then we need to feed our hearts the right kinds of things.

The same thing is true with food isn't it? People who eat only junk food aren't as strong as those who eat healthy. Let's eat some snack today that will help us to be healthy in our bodies.

Snack Idea

Preparation: Choose a healthy snack like yogurt covered raisins, cut apple wedges, cheese, or grapes.

Use the opportunity to talk about how what people eat can make them strong. Everyday people make choices about their food. In the same way, healthy relating habits will help you grow in kindness. It takes small steps of kindness each day to become a person who is strong on the inside.

● ● ● ● ●

Review and Close

Let's talk about some ways that you can show kindness in your family. How might you show kindness to your mom? Your dad? Your brother? Your sister? Your grandma or grandpa? Can you think of a time when you were kind to someone but it was hard to do? Use this as a brainstorming time to help children understand how to practically apply the things they're learning about kindness.

What was the most important lesson that Saul of Tarsus learned from his experience on the road to Damascus? Was it that God is in charge? Or that God wanted to have Saul working for him? Those

are important lessons and when Saul decided to follow God, it changed the way he treated other people. He wasn't mean to Christians anymore.

Sometimes children treat other kids in a mean way because they are different. They look different or talk different. Marcy had a problem. She had only one arm. When she was born her other arm was missing. Marcy told this story:

"It's hard to live with just one arm. I have to do things differently than others. You'd be surprised how many times you use two hands to do something and I only have one. But the hardest thing is when people aren't kind to me or make fun of me. I can't help it that I only have one arm. I'm trying the best I can. Sometimes kids laugh at me. That hurts me a lot.

But there are some kids who are kind to me. They don't pay attention to the fact that I only have one arm. They know that I'm just another kid and I can have fun, talk about things, and be friends with people. When kids are kind to me then it makes me feel good. I like that and I respect those people. When kids are mean to me I know that they have problems. It makes me angry sometimes, but mostly I feel sad because I realize that their problem is worse than mine."

Boys and girls, what are we learning about kindness? Yes, we're learning that kind people are strong on the inside. What are we learning about meanness? Yes, mean people are weak on the inside. Let's look for ways that we all can be strong on the inside. Kindness is like a treasure. It's powerful. It's special, and it's valuable.

Welcome Activity
Binoculars

I Once Was Blind

But Now I See

Activity
Optical
Illusions

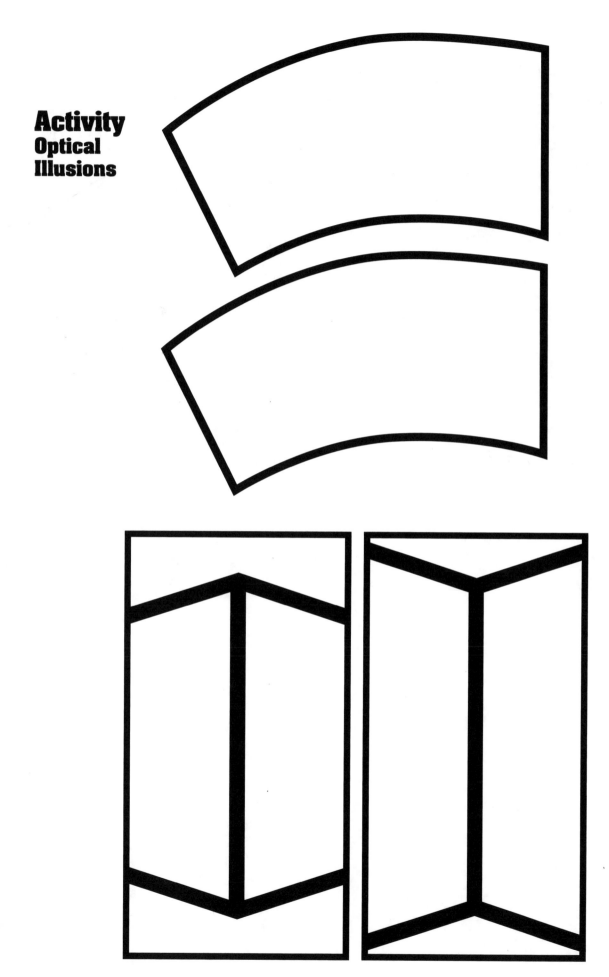

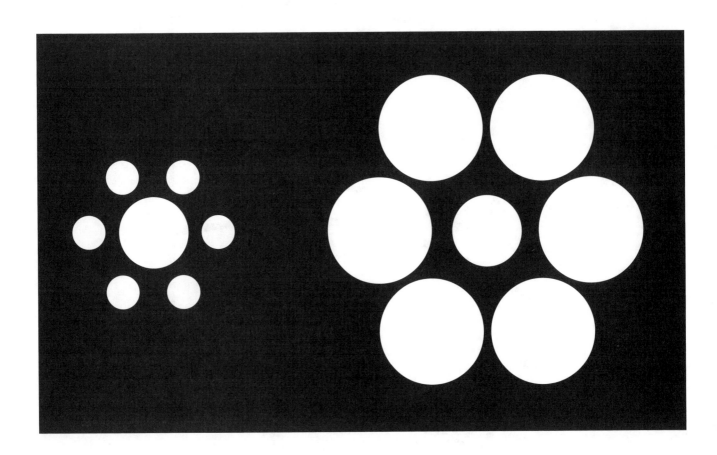

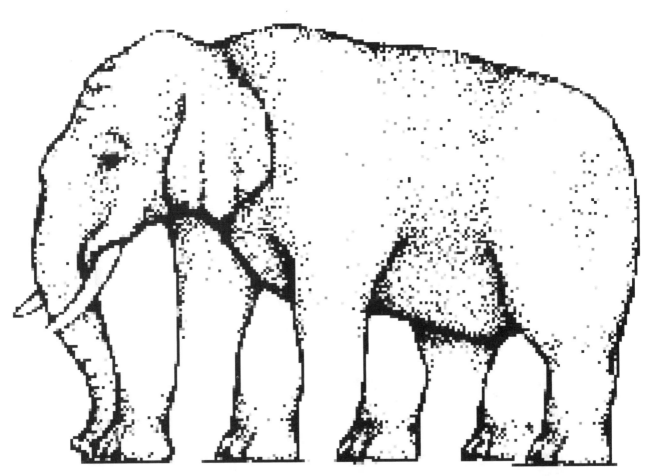

76 Hopatcong Drive, Lawrenceville, NJ 08648-4136
(800) 771-8334 or (609) 771-8002
Email: parent@biblicalparenting.org
Web: biblicalparenting.org

Changing What Children Believe

Dear Parent,

Children often believe strange things in their hearts and those beliefs effect the way they act, talk, and treat other people. Helping children change on a heart level is part of our goal as parents. It means that we must help mold the things our children believe.

Theme: Kind people are strong on the inside.

In this lesson we've taken a common mis-belief among children and tried to help kids see things from a different perspective. Children often believe that meanness is a sign of strength and that kind people are weak. Of course we know that really the opposite is true.

In this lesson we played games, told stories, and had activities that give children a different way to think about life. Saul of Tarsus in our Bible story was mean to God's people for a long time until God got a hold of his heart and changed what he believed. That made all the difference in the world as God revealed the truth that kindness to everyone is more important. Philippians 4:13 was our Bible verse emphasizing the Lord's strength in us.

You might ask your child how a piece of paper can hold a glass of water. Or what the difference is between a tug of war and a tug of kindness.

As you interact with your child this week reinforce this theme. Children don't usually change instantly. They need a multi-faceted approach to touch the heart. Pray with your child about ways you might show kindness to others. Talk about how it takes strength on the inside to be kind and about how you feel when someone is kind to you. Practice kindness as a family this week. Some concentrated work in this area will help children change what they believe.

Blessings,

Scott Turansky   Joanne Miller
National Center for Biblical Parenting
www.biblicalparenting.org

What is Heart Change All About?

Preparing Your Heart to Teach Session 3

One of the enemies of clear thinking and right responses is frustration and anger. Anger can blur one's ability to stay calm and handle a problem carefully. What do you do when you start to get a little excited or upset? How do you get yourself back to a place where you have enough peace to handle life's challenges?

Your maturity in this area allows you to meet frustrations without resorting to meanness, sarcasm, disrespect, and unkindness. Most children have a difficult time in this area. They lack the skills necessary to respond graciously when they're corrected or given a no answer. Kids resort to all kinds of manipulations to express their disapproval.

But it's not just a kid problem is it? As adults, we often react out of our own selfishness when we get upset. The solution is to learn to handle our emotions in more constructive ways and not allow them to get us riled up. That solution is the topic of this lesson. As you help children learn to settle down, take a moment and apply the same truths to your own life. It's a challenge we all need.

What Children Learn in Session 3

In this lesson children will learn about a tool we call a Break. A Break is simply going to a quiet place to settle down before returning to debrief with a parent or teacher. Unlike Time Out, a Break focuses on the heart and puts the responsibility for change onto the child. When the child is ready to talk calmly about the problem, then he or she can initiate back.

Theme: When I'm upset I can stop, settle down, and change my heart.

Kids will gain a greater understanding of why they need a Break and they'll even practice it. Using the story of Jonah along with several activities and a craft, kids will explore the value of taking a Break and learn how to implement it in family life.

Read Along in the Book, "Parenting is Heart Work"

Correction is foundational to any parenting strategy. In fact, God values correction as he works with his children. Over and over again, God corrected people in the scriptures. He wanted heart change and he called it repentance. Chapter 14 takes apart the biblical concept of repentance and defines it in practical terms. It then offers hands-on tools for helping children change their hearts, not just their behavior. Chapter 15 discusses how a Break can be an excellent parenting tool to touch the heart. In particular, the Break transfers the responsibility for change to the child, a welcome concept in most homes.

Session 3

Theme

When I'm upset I can stop, settle down, and change my heart.

Welcome Activity
Heart Mosaic

Preparation: Photocopy onto cardstock the heart template at the end of this lesson. Also photocopy the instructions page on regular paper. Cut sheets of construction paper into approximately 3x4 inch pieces. Have glue available.

Children can take the colored construction paper pieces, tear them into smaller pieces, and then glue them onto their base in the shape of a heart. This project uses color and texture to demonstrate creativity.

Tell the kids that this craft illustrates the fact that many things are in the heart. The heart is the place where we feel upset at times. When we don't like what happened or it's frustrating, we feel it in our hearts. The heart is also the place where we can be stubborn. I know that sometimes I want something that I can't have, and that's a challenge for my heart. But the heart is also the place where we feel at peace. Sometimes it takes some work to change our hearts from being upset to being more calm. Today we're going to talk about the heart, especially when parents correct you. Sometimes children get pretty upset when corrected by Mom or Dad. One of the things that helps kids be successful in those moments is to stop, settle down, and change your heart.

Have children place their Heart Mosaic along the wall or in a safe place before continuing. They'll add to this pile as the session unfolds.

For Younger Children
You may want to cut the construction paper into strips so they can easily tear pieces.

Transition

This next activity is a visual demonstration so everyone needs to be in a place where they can see. One of the ways that kids learn how to stop, settle down, and change the heart is through what we call a Break. This activity illustrates what happens in a child's heart when the child goes to take a Break.

Together Time

Use the ideas below along with your own thoughts and the Bible to dialogue with the children and help them see that having a calm heart is most important even when things around you are upsetting.

Object Lesson
Colored Water Turns Clear with a Break

Preparation: This activity works because of a chemical reaction, so be sure to follow the directions carefully and measure the amounts of the liquids accurately. Before class, put five drops of red food coloring on a spoon and blow it dry with a hair dryer. This usually takes about five minutes of hot air before it dries. Turn the spoon upside down and place it on the table so children can't see the food coloring. Have three glasses on the table. The first one contains four ounces of water. The second glass contains one tbsp of vinegar. In a third glass put two tbsps of bleach. Put a piece of colored construction paper on one side of the table.

Move the first glass to the front of the table and tell the children, "Let's imagine that this glass of water is your heart. A lot of things happen in the heart but one of the things we want to talk about is how we feel in our hearts. Sometimes when we get upset we don't handle problems very well."

Pick up the glass with vinegar in it and allow children to smell it. Say, "We'll pretend that this liquid represents problems we face in life. It doesn't look like a problem. It's clear like the water, but smell it. Does it smell like water? Let's add these problems to the heart and see what happens." Build the excitement and anticipation and watch children's faces as you combine two liquids together and nothing happens. Of course, at first, nothing happens until you pick up the spoon and stir the liquids together and the food coloring turns the water red. Stir for only about one second and put the spoon down on the table to use again.

Continue by saying, "Parents sometimes give kids instructions that they'd rather not do. Or they say no to a child's request, or sometimes parents have to correct kids. When that happens kids can get pretty upset and the correction and limits create problems inside the heart in the same way that this water has turned red. Children then sometimes say mean things to parents or they are disrespectful or they just say no. The problem is in the heart.

"What the child needs to do is stop, settle down, and change the heart. We call that a Break. Kids sometimes need to take a Break in order to stop, settle down, and change the heart." So, I'm going to move the glass onto the piece of construction paper where the heart is now taking a Break. Amazing things happen when kids take a Break. The heart begins to change. A Break is a great place for adults too, so this isn't just a kid solution. When the heart gets upset, it needs to stop, settle down and change." Pour the bleach into the water and watch the color disappear gradually in about 10 seconds. The color slowly dissipates right before your eyes. The Break helped settle the heart. Now the glass isn't colored anymore. In the same way, children go take a Break and then they return ready to solve problems and do the right thing.

Move the glass back to the center of the table away from the Break place. Take the spoon and stir the water again and it will turn red. Quickly put the glass back onto the Break place and within 10 seconds it will turn back to clear.

"Sometimes children must go back to the Break a few times before they can really settle down." You can repeat this 3-4 times or until the food coloring is all gone off the spoon.

Bible Story
"Jonah, It's Break Time"

I'd like to tell you a Bible story. It's one I think you've heard, but I don't think you've heard it quite this way before. How many of you have heard the story of Jonah? Yes, I see that most of you have. Listen to me tell it and see if you can understand this idea of the Break.

Have you ever been in a grocery store, at the park, or even at church and you hear a mom call her little boy and instead of coming, he runs the other way? At first it looks funny but then you see the mom getting angry and you say to yourself "Uh oh, trouble is coming!" A story like that happened in the Bible.

Jonah ran the other way when God told him to go to Nineveh. Jonah was just like a three-year-old in a grocery store and he tried to run away from God. Now, God could have just picked up Jonah by the back of the collar and said, "You are going to Nineveh" and put him on the road. But God didn't do that. Do you know why?

God is interested in the heart. The heart is the place where we make choices. It's the place where we decide what's right to do, even if we don't feel like it. The heart is the place where our attitudes are developed and where we feel things. God wanted Jonah to change his heart. You see, Jonah was being selfish. He didn't want to go and talk to the people of Nineveh. His heart was just thinking about himself. So he ran away from God.

Now God said to himself, "I'm going to have to discipline this man. What

technique should I use? I want something that will help him change his heart….
I know! I'll use a Break."

Let me explain to you, boys and girls, what a Break is. The Break is a place where you sit for a bit and stop, settle down, and change your heart before you can continue in life. In fact, I want someone to demonstrate this for me.
Who would like to be my volunteer? (Have your volunteer stand up and come close to you.) Now the first thing we have to do is imagine that you did something wrong. Boys and girls, what do you think we could pretend that our volunteer did wrong? (Choose an offense like hitting or grabbing from a brother or sister, or complaining when a parent gives an instruction.) You hit your brother! (Express shock but not anger.) You need to go over near the table over there and sit on the floor and take a Break. Now while you're there, I want you to stop, settle down, and change your heart and then you come back to me when you're ready. (Allow the child to go and sit down and then you might have to coax him or her out of the Break.) When the child comes back, simply say, "Do you know what you did wrong? Okay let's try to do the right thing next time. Thank you."

Have a second volunteer demonstrate the Break. Remember that the Break works in part because the child initiates the return demonstrating a change of heart, so try to have the child return without prompting. Usually, clear instructions followed by silence motivate the child to return, but you may have to say to the other children, "Let's see Billy return to me with a changed heart."

God said, "What technique should I use to discipline this guy? I know, I'll use a Break. Where should I have him sit? I know, I'll create a fish. So God had a great big fish come up along side of the boat and they threw Jonah overboard. Jonah got swallowed by that fish. Now, boys and girls, if you got swallowed by a big fish how long would it take you to change your heart? About one minute, or one second, right? I'd want to get out of that fish right away.

Did you know it took Jonah three days to change his heart? I hope it doesn't take you that long to change your heart. Sometimes kids go to the Break and they are angry and they say things like, "It's not fair. I can't believe I have to sit in this place. I don't like it when you tell me what to do. Why do I always get into trouble?" And on and on it goes for a while. Those kids need to stay in the Break for a longer time. They aren't ready to come out and if they come out too early then they just fight with their parents or with their friends or brothers and sisters. The Break is a place to stop, settle down, and change your heart.

God knew that Jonah had changed his heart and that he was ready to obey, so he commanded the fish to throw up, and the fish did! He threw up Jonah right onto the land. Jonah chapter 3 tells us that God told Jonah again to go to Nineveh, and then it says this: "And Jonah obeyed." I like that verse. What do you think God would have done if Jonah hadn't obeyed? You see, obeying is a sign of a heart that's right. God is interested in the heart. This time God used a big fish to help Jonah change his heart. If you were God and Jonah didn't obey this time, what other things could you make happen that might motivate Jonah to change his heart? (Talk about things like creepy bugs, violent storms, lightning, and tornados that God might use to get Jonah's attention.)

Boys and girls, your parents want to see your heart change too. They don't just want to see you change your behavior. Sometimes they may use a Break to help you stop, settle down, and change your heart. If that doesn't work, they have lots of other ideas for helping you change your heart. I don't think you want to see those things. It's best to just respond to a Break.

I like a Break because it's an adult way to respond to correction. Sometimes as an adult when I realize I've done the wrong thing, I just need to take a Break, stop, settle down, and change my heart so that I can work on doing the right thing. You might encourage your mom and dad to discipline you with a Break. It's a much better way to correct kids than what sometimes happens in families. And then you need to be able to respond to the Break so that it will work. If you do this you will grow much faster and be much more successful at handling problems, mistakes, and conflict in life.

We have a Bible verse that helps us remember this idea. The verse comes in 1 Samuel 16:7 and it tells us what's most important to God.

This Bible story was taken from Jonah 1-3.

Bible Verse

1 Samuel 16:7
"Man looks at the outward appearance, but the Lord looks at the heart."

● ● ● ● ———————————

Transition

I want you to remember the story about Jonah. I'm sure you've heard it before. But I want you to remember how important a Break is in changing the heart, so we're going to have some fun making a big fish. Demonstrate to children the finished craft and how you suck Jonah right into the mouth.

Craft
The Big Fish Catches Jonah

Preparation: From a party store, purchase the party favors that unroll when you blow into them and the "tongue" retracts when you stop blowing. These are typically called "blowouts." Photocopy the little Jonah at the end of this lesson. You'll also need yarn, tape, markers or ball point pens, and one styrofoam cup for each child.

Don't distribute the party favors until the children have done the rest of the craft so that the kids

don't get distracted by blowing on them. Have each child break out the bottom of a Styrofoam cup. Using markers or ball point pens, have each child draw scales on the fish and put eyes on either side so that the smaller end of the cup is the mouth. Tape the party favor along the inside of the cup with the "tongue" ready to expand out the bottom of the cup.

Create the Jonah using the template at the end of this lesson. Tape or glue a piece of yarn about 12″ long to the back of Jonah's head. After creating all the pieces, have children sit on the floor around the table, put a weight like a book or a piece of tape on the yarn to hold it on the table and dangle Jonah over the table as if cast into the sea. Have each child blow into his or her party favor so the tongue comes out of the fish's mouth and tries to grab Jonah and suck him right into the fish's mouth. After Jonah takes a Break, they can have the fish throw up Jonah onto the land on top of the table.

Kids will have fun with this craft and will never forget the story of Jonah and the big fish. Be sure to take pictures for your photo diary. Don't allow children to play with these toys too long because the blowouts aren't very sturdy and may break easily. After the craft time have the children put their Jonah and fish on their Heart Mosaic and then sit back down and get ready for the race.

● ● ● ● ● ———————————

Transition

Who can tell me why someone would have to sit and take a Break? Yes, because they are upset and need to stop, settle down, and change the heart. Sometimes kids try to continue on and solve problems or they react because they're upset and they really need to just stop, settle down, and change the heart. We're now going to play a game that will help us remember that sometimes we need to start over. It's better to slow down sometimes in order to be more effective.

Session 3

Activity
The Race

Preparation:

You'll need two teaspoons and two potatoes for older children. Use two teaspoons and two grapes for younger children.

Prepare an obstacle course using four or five chairs forcing children to go to the other end of the room and back, navigating around the chairs. For older children you may make the race interesting by having the children cross each other's path forcing them to navigate around each other. Give each older racer a teaspoon and a potato. By putting one hand behind the back, race through the course. If the child drops the potato or tries to hold it on, then have that child start all over again.

With young children you may want to use a grape in the spoon and not actually race but have each child go one at a time trying to accomplish the task.

Most children will struggle with this activity and have to return to the beginning several times. Life is like that. Frustrations often mean that we have to start over. You may even see that frustration in the game. If so, you might remove the competitive edge by having all the children sit down and let's see if anyone can make it through the whole course without dropping the potato. Usually a child, when settled down and careful, can complete the course without dropping the potato. Use this event to talk about how family life can get hectic sometimes. You want to get some things done or you just want to play a game or watch a movie but then Mom or Dad asks for something to be done. It's easy to get upset but important to remain calm. How do you do that? Maybe you can just take a deep breath, but sometimes you'll have to take a Break to settle down and be ready to be more successful.

Transition

What does a Break help someone do? Stop, settle down, and change the heart. Let's talk about what it means to change the heart a little bit. The heart can be a place where we get upset, angry, and even stubborn sometimes. The Break gives a child some time to settle down. Change is important. How long does it take for a person to change the heart? Sometimes it only takes a few seconds and a person is ready to return. Other times it may take 20 minutes or an hour, depending how upset a child is.

One of the signs that someone is growing up is that they can change more quickly. The person who isn't mature often has to take much longer to make the changes necessary to reenter family life. It's interesting how a person's heart can change from one thing one minute to something completely different the next. A Break often allows a person to change what's in the heart.

Snack
Buried Treasure Mini Muffins

Preparation: Bake or buy mini-muffins. Using a knife, gently insert the photocopied treasure slips at the end of this lesson. Leave a small tail hanging out.

Serve the mini-muffins and have children take out the slips of paper and read what they say. Talk about the hidden treasure of settling down in a Break.

Transition

Who can tell me what happens when a child takes a Break? Stop, settle down, and change the heart. In fact, a Break is really a treasure in family life. It does some great things to help people stay calm and work out problems without getting upset and losing control. I want to show you that the Break is a treasure as we do this next activity.

Activity
Treasure Cave

Preparation: Create a Treasure Cave by placing three chairs next to each other in one row. Then create a second row of chairs behind the first, facing the opposite direction about three feet apart. Put a blanket over the chairs to form a cave that children will go into. Place a treat inside the cave. That treat may be some chocolate coins, candy, or stickers that children would enjoy.

Tell kids that this is a Break place and that taking a Break is like finding hidden treasure. You want to demonstrate this by having children enter the cave unhappy and exit the cave happy. Who would like to go first? Show me your pouting face going in and let's see a happy face when you come out. Have children enter the cave one at a time to get their treat. Instruct them to take one piece of hidden treasure when they take a Break.

Review and Close

The Break isn't an easy thing to learn in family life, but it's worth the work. It takes practice and self-control. Sometimes children get angry or upset and they need to take a Break so they can stop, settle down, and change their hearts.

Let's talk about some times when kids tend to get upset. What are those times? Let children respond with ideas. Kids get upset when they are corrected. For example, Jack was teasing his little sister. Mom said, "Jack please stop teasing your sister." Jack got angry and said, "She's just a tattle tale." Mom said, "Jack, I'd like you to take a Break and then come back and see me. When children are corrected they benefit from a Break.

Chrissy wanted to go over to her friend's house but Mom said, "No, we're not going to do that this afternoon." Chrissy got mad and started stomping around and yelling. Mom said, "Chrissy, I want you to take a Break in the hall and come back and see me when you're ready." Boys and girls, how do you think Mom will know when Chrissy is ready? That's right, she'll be settled down and her heart will be changed. Everyone will be able to tell because she won't be pouting and angry. She'll be ready to talk about the problem.

When do you think it would be helpful for you to take a Break in family life? Allow children to share possible scenarios when a Break might be helpful. Help kids make the personal application to their own families. If children are reluctant to share or can't think of how to apply it, share another example or two about how a Break might be effective to help a child be ready to work on a problem.

Pray and thank the Lord for the heart. Ask God to help children this week to have hearts that are calm instead of upset.

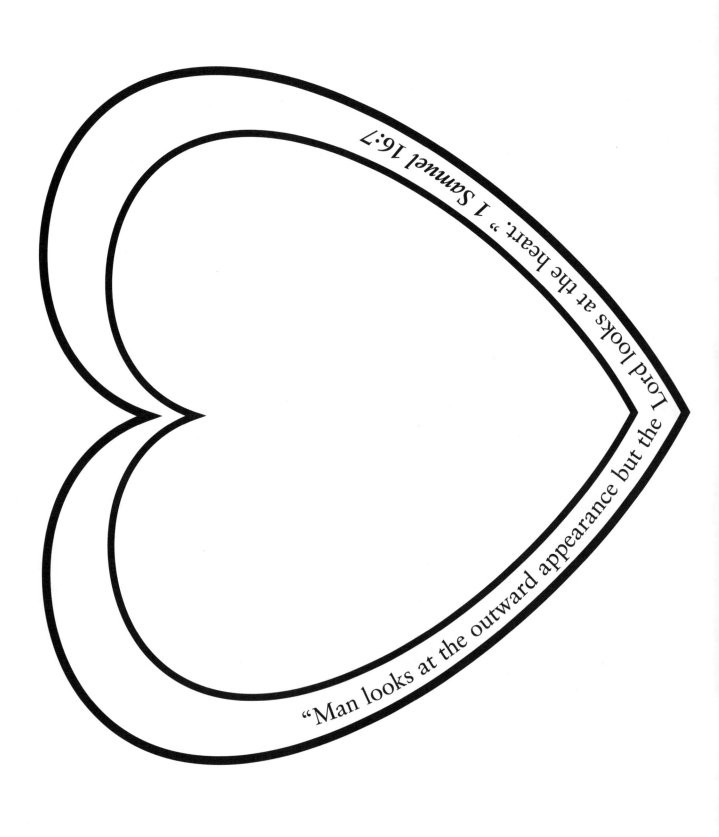

"Man looks at the outward appearance but the Lord looks at the heart." 1 Samuel 16:7

Heart Mosaic
Instructions for older children

1 Choose a piece of colored construction paper as your base.

2 Choose smaller pieces of construction paper for your mosaic.

3 Rip the smaller pieces.

4 Glue the smaller pieces on your page in the shape of a heart.

"Man looks at the outward appearance but the Lord looks at the heart." 1 Samuel 16:7

Session 3

Craft
The Big Fish Catches Jonah

Snack
Buried Treasure Mini Muffins

A Break Helps the Heart Settle Down	A Break Helps the Heart Settle Down	A Break Helps the Heart Settle Down
A Break Helps the Heart Settle Down	A Break Helps the Heart Settle Down	A Break Helps the Heart Settle Down
A Break Helps the Heart Settle Down	A Break Helps the Heart Settle Down	A Break Helps the Heart Settle Down
A Break Helps the Heart Settle Down	A Break Helps the Heart Settle Down	A Break Helps the Heart Settle Down
A Break Helps the Heart Settle Down	A Break Helps the Heart Settle Down	A Break Helps the Heart Settle Down
A Break Helps the Heart Settle Down	A Break Helps the Heart Settle Down	A Break Helps the Heart Settle Down
A Break Helps the Heart Settle Down	A Break Helps the Heart Settle Down	A Break Helps the Heart Settle Down
A Break Helps the Heart Settle Down	A Break Helps the Heart Settle Down	A Break Helps the Heart Settle Down
A Break Helps the Heart Settle Down	A Break Helps the Heart Settle Down	A Break Helps the Heart Settle Down
A Break Helps the Heart Settle Down	A Break Helps the Heart Settle Down	A Break Helps the Heart Settle Down
A Break Helps the Heart Settle Down	A Break Helps the Heart Settle Down	A Break Helps the Heart Settle Down
A Break Helps the Heart Settle Down	A Break Helps the Heart Settle Down	A Break Helps the Heart Settle Down
A Break Helps the Heart Settle Down	A Break Helps the Heart Settle Down	A Break Helps the Heart Settle Down
A Break Helps the Heart Settle Down	A Break Helps the Heart Settle Down	A Break Helps the Heart Settle Down
A Break Helps the Heart Settle Down	A Break Helps the Heart Settle Down	A Break Helps the Heart Settle Down
A Break Helps the Heart Settle Down	A Break Helps the Heart Settle Down	A Break Helps the Heart Settle Down

76 Hopatcong Drive, Lawrenceville, NJ 08648-4136
(800) 771-8334 or (609) 771-8002
Email: parent@biblicalparenting.org
Web: biblicalparenting.org

A Heart-Based Approach for Correcting Children

Dear Parent,

It would be nice if children always did what they're supposed to do but that doesn't happen. Children need correction and they need parents who can correct them in ways that touch the heart. Only when children change their hearts can lasting change take place.

Now it is true that you can't force a change of heart, but you *can* influence this deeper work. In today's lesson your child learned about a Break. The Break is a tool that parents can use to teach children how to stop, settle down, and be willing to work on the problem.

Theme: When I'm upset I can stop, settle down, and change my heart.

Using role-play, games, activities, and a Bible story, your child heard how important it is to change the heart. The story of Jonah illustrates the Break well. Jonah was doing the wrong thing. God chose to discipline him. What technique did God choose? It was a Break, having Jonah sit for a bit and consider his ways. The approach was successful because Jonah changed his heart and then obeyed.

We used the Bible verse, 1 Samuel 16:7 to talk about the importance of the heart and how God sees and values it. You might ask your child about the race with the spoon or the colored water that turned clear.

It takes time to develop a Break as a routine that you can use in correction, but the work you do now to develop a good pattern will go a long way. One of the advantages of the Break is that it shifts the responsibility for a change of heart to the child instead of the parent. Only when the child has settled down and is ready to work on the problem can he or she initiate and return to the parent for a discussion about the problem, and then re-enter family life.

The Break helps settle emotions before dialogue instead of watching the intensity escalate into an emotional battle. Most importantly though, over time kids learn how to discipline themselves. A Break is an adult skill and many parents would benefit from putting it into practice in their own lives.

Spend time this week talking about heart change when you correct your child. You want your child to think differently about the correction process and about ways he or she can learn from discipline instead of fighting against it.

Blessings,

Scott Turansky   Joanne Miller
National Center for Biblical Parenting
www.biblicalparenting.org

Correction is Like Buried Treasure

Preparing Your Heart to Teach Session 4

How do you, as an adult, respond when someone corrects you? Some people tend to blame others, or rationalize, or defend themselves. What we all need is a healthy dose of humility, allowing us to learn from others. Unfortunately, sometimes other people rub it in or correct us in harsh or demeaning ways, diminishing any positive response we might have considered.

God tells us that correction is valuable, not just for children, but for all of us. Proverbs 12:1 says, "Whoever loves discipline loves knowledge, but he who hates correction is stupid."

Correction allows us to learn from life, grow more quickly, and see blind spots and weaknesses that we tend to overlook. Correction often happens in family life when wives or husbands make observations. Sometimes the kids correct us with an innocent comment or a hurt look on their faces.

The person who can accept correction learns faster and is often appreciated by others. But many people view correction as an attack, challenging the foundation of their being. Many of these people have built a wall around themselves warning people that they had better not even try to correct them lest they experience a vengeful anger.

Take some time this week and examine your own heart when you're corrected. Are you willing to allow people to evaluate you, point out things that need to change, or correct your mistakes? If you are, then you're well on your way to growing in wisdom. After all, God often uses the people we know best and love the most as tools of correction in our lives. They are gifts that help us learn and grow.

What Children Learn in Session 4

Receiving correction is a great treasure because it allows children to mature more quickly and develop the wisdom they need to be successful in life.

Unfortunately, most children view correction as an attack and they use all kinds of techniques to defend themselves against it.

Theme: Correction is valuable because it helps me learn and grow.

In this session children will do several activities and listen to a fun story about the value of correction. They'll learn that God uses even simple things like Balaam's donkey to correct his children. Some people have problems, because they don't like correction.

Read Along in the Book, "Parenting is Heart Work"

Sometimes when people talk about the heart they assume that God only changes hearts directly, but Chapter 10 explores the value of parental teaching in helping children adjust what they believe. Lecturing is different than teaching and expressing your viewpoint is different than touching a child on a heart level. Chapter 13 discusses the value of correction and how and why correction works in anyone's life. Unfortunately children often devalue correction or see it as an enemy. It takes work to correct children, and of course the way it's done can greatly influence its effectiveness.

Session 4

Theme

Correction is valuable because it helps me learn and grow.

Welcome Activity
Treasure Chest

Preparation: In advance obtain empty tissue (Kleenex) boxes that have an opening only at the top, one for each student. Cut along three side with an exacto knife leaving a "hinge" at the back for the box to open. This cut should be about 3/4 inches down from the top. Depending on how the boxes are made, you may need to staple the lids to keep the pieces together. The "hinge" is made by bending the box lid back and creating a fold along the back, 3/4 inches down from the top. Photocopy the Treasure Chest page at the end of this lesson. Provide construction paper, scissors, glue, brads, and rubber bands.

Have children trace the top of the box onto a piece of construction paper, cut it out and then glue it on the top of their box. Then glue the sign on top of the construction paper. The color of the construction paper should match the rest of the box as much as possible. Cut out and glue the handles and the lock onto the box. Poke a hole in the lid and the base in the front of the box and push a brad through each hole. Use a rubber band or twisty tie to hold the box shut.

While children are working on their Treasure Chest, see if they can remember the message from the last lesson. Remember today's lesson is the second of three that focus on correction. The point of this lesson is that correction is valuable because it helps us learn and grow.

Together Time

Use the ideas below along with your own thoughts and the Bible to dialogue with the children and help them see that correction isn't something to be feared or resisted. Correction helps a person learn and grow.

Object Lesson
The Flashlight that Won't Work

Preparation: Prepare a flashlight in advance by folding a dollar bill and placing it inside the flashlight, at the bottom, preventing the electrical contacts from touching the battery. Put one of the batteries in the wrong way.

When the children have gathered together pull out your flashlight and say, "This is my flashlight. How many of you have a flashlight? What are some things you use a flashlight for? I use my flashlight when I have to look under the refrigerator or go out to the shed."

Try to turn on your flashlight. Of course it won't work so shake it and tap it on the floor to try to get it to turn on. Act frustrated and embarrassed about your flashlight that doesn't work.

"Let me see what's wrong here."

Open the flashlight and take out the batteries and discover the first problem.

"Oh, here it is. I guess I just didn't do it right. Well, now we have it all fixed up and I can go on with my story. I was saying that this is my favorite flashlight and when I turn it on like this…"

Of course, it doesn't work again so again you're frustrated and embarrassed.

"What could be the problem here? This flashlight worked yesterday just fine. I was planning to share this story with you but now my flashlight isn't working. What could be the problem here?"

Take the flashlight apart again and look inside and then tap the flashlight to get the dollar bill out of the bottom.

"What is a dollar doing in my flashlight? This isn't a bank. Someone must be trying to use my flashlight as a piggy bank. No wonder it isn't working. Well, let's put it all back together now and see if it works. As I was saying, this is my favorite flashlight and when I turn it on like this… it works."

You know boys and girls, this flashlight reminds me of people sometimes. They think they've done everything right but for some reason things just aren't working for them. They have to find out what the problem is and correct it before things will be better. Correction is an important part of life. If we don't listen to correction then things don't work well for us. Correction is valuable because it helps us learn and grow.

Bible Story
Balaam and the Talking Donkey

How many of you have ever ridden a pony or a horse? Have any of you ever ridden a donkey? When you ride a horse you have to be careful. The horse might go right under a tree branch but if you're not careful, you'll get hit by the branch. So you have to guide the horse or the pony or the donkey in the right way.

Today I want to tell you an amazing story about a man who rode a donkey. His name was Balaam and he was a prophet. When God spoke to someone he would often speak through one of the prophets. God would tell the prophet what to say and the prophet would say it to the person.

One day, the bad king of Moab sent messengers to the prophet and said, "I would like you to put a curse on God's people."

Oh no. What would Balaam do? "Wait here," he said to the messengers. "I will go ask God what he wants to do." So Balaam talked to God about it.

"Do not put a curse on my people," God said. "They are blessed."

So Balaam went back and told the messengers, "I'm sorry, but I can't put a curse on God's people. God says no."

So the messengers returned to the bad king and they gave their report. The bad king was not happy. He sent some more messengers with the promise that Balaam would receive lots of money if he would just put a curse on God's people.

Oh no. What do you think Balaam is going to do? Should he take all the money? He would be rich. No. He said to the messengers, "Even if you give me a whole palace filled with silver and gold, I can't do anything unless God says. But you wait here. I'll go talk to God again and see what he says."

Balaam knew that God didn't want him to curse his people, but he asked again anyway. After all the messengers were offering him a lot of money. So God said, "Ok, go ahead but only say what I tell you to say." God was not happy with Balaam who wanted to get this money.

The next morning Balaam put a saddle on his donkey. He got on it and started riding toward the bad king of Moab. On the way, the donkey saw an angel of the Lord standing there with a sword ready to kill Balaam. Well, the donkey knew that continuing to go forward would mean sure death for both her and her master. So the donkey went right off the road into a field.

Balaam was mad. He got a stick and beat the donkey to get her back on the road. A little while later, the donkey saw the angel of the Lord again. This time they were trying to get through a narrow place in the road between two walls. The donkey knew that they couldn't get through without getting killed by the angel so the donkey pushed very close to the wall and smashed Balaam's foot against the wall.

Balaam was angry so he beat the poor donkey again, and they started down the road another time. This time the donkey saw the angel in a small part of the road and there was no place to turn. So the donkey just stopped and lay down right there in the road.

Balaam was very angry with his donkey. "You cottin-pickin', good for nothin', low-down donkey. Take that!! I'll kill you and feed you to the vultures."

Just then God did an amazing thing while Balaam was having his temper tantrum. He made the donkey talk. Can you believe that? A talking donkey. She said, "Why are you beating me these three times? What did I do wrong?"

Now what would you do if you heard a donkey talking? I think I might get out of there quick. But not Balaam. He was so angry he started talking back to the donkey. They must have looked funny, the two of them talking together.

Balaam said, "You have made a fool of me. If I had a sword, I'd kill you right now."

The donkey spoke again and said, "I have been your donkey for a long time. I've never treated you poorly. I've always done what you asked. Have I ever done this to you before?"

"No," said Balaam. Just then God opened Balaam's eyes and he too saw the angel of the Lord with his sword up in the air ready to kill him. Balaam was shocked and he felt so bad. He realized that he should have known that there was a problem. Balaam should have seen the indications that he was doing the wrong thing. But he didn't.

Balaam's problem was that he couldn't receive correction well. He had his own ideas of what he wanted to do and he wasn't willing to listen to anyone else. God taught Balaam a very important lesson that day, to listen and do the right thing. Even if someone offers you a lot of money to do the wrong thing, never do it.

What do you think Balaam did for his donkey after that? I'm sure he gave the donkey a special treat and if the donkey ever did something strange again, I'm sure that Balaam was very careful to treat the donkey in a kind way.

It's important for all of us to listen to correction. Sometimes we may not understand it but God does good things in our lives when we receive correction well.

(Hold up your flashlight) I've talked to you about a flashlight and about correction. They both have something in common. They show us the right way to go. Correction is valuable because it helps us learn and grow. There's a verse in the Bible that puts these two ideas together too, a flashlight, or a lamp, and the idea of correction.

For Younger Children

The Bible story in all its detail is quite complicated for young children to understand so simplify it by addressing the main points. A man was going to do the wrong thing. A donkey saw an angel and talked. The man didn't listen. We need to listen to moms and dads.

This Bible story was taken from Numbers 22.

Bible Verse

Proverbs 6:23
"For these commands are a lamp, this teaching is a light, and the corrections of discipline are the way to life."

● ● ● ● ●

Transition

Why is correction valuable? Yes, because it helps us learn and grow. Who thinks they can make a paper airplane that will fly the farthest? In this next activity we're going to all try to make airplanes. Then we'll try to fly them. Then we'll each make a second airplane, correcting some of the things we think would make ours better. We're doing this because correction helps us learn. Sometimes we think we have a good way to do something but then it needs correction.

Craft (For Older Children)
Airplane Racers

Preparation: Have plenty of 8 1/2" x 11" paper available for your students.

Ask them to each design a paper airplane that they will use for a contest. Have the children spend time sitting down at tables to design their planes. A plane could have large or narrow wings, be long or short, or have a sharp or blunt nose. Children should also be encouraged to create flaps on the wings to guide the plane. Some children may not know how

to make a paper airplane. In that case you may want to walk them through the process of a simple airplane.

After the children have designed their planes, have them stand behind a line and try to "land" their planes inside a circle 15 feet away or onto a table just a few feet away. After the first few attempts, send the children back to the tables to create another one or adjust their airplanes. They can learn from others' ideas or just from their own experience. This is a form of correction as children try to hone in on the perfect airplane to land on the runway.

Have the children sit down and set their airplanes down on the table or floor so they aren't distracted by them during a short debriefing. Boys and girls, what kind of changes did you make to your second airplane to get it to go farther? That's correction. Correction helps us do better. Sometimes moms and dads correct kids because they see that they're making a mistake that will hinder them. They see a bad attitude, or unkind-ness, or disrespect and parents know that if kids grow up that way they will be unhappy and unsuccessful. Parents correct kids to help them learn and grow.

Craft (For Younger Children)
The Wise Donkey

Preparation: Photocopy the Wise Donkey Craft onto cardstock. Each child will need a small paper bag and crayons. Cut out the donkey pieces ahead of time. Have children color the donkey pieces and then glue the pieces onto a small lunch bag. You may want to take a picture for your photo diary. Set the puppets aside to dry and let children take them home to remind them of the wise donkey in the story.

Boys and girls, do you know what we learn from the story of the donkey? We learn how important it is to listen to correction. If Mom says, "Billy, stop playing so rough with the baby," Billy needs to stop right away and be corrected. How do you respond to correction? Do you respond with "Okay Mom," or "Okay Dad?" That's a good response to correction isn't it. Some kids respond by pouting or getting angry like Balaam did in the story. That doesn't help. We want to respond well to correction so that we can learn and grow.

● ● ● ● ● ─────────────

Transition

Correction is important because it helps us change our hearts. The heart is a pretty complicated place sometimes, but as it changes some great things happen. This next activity is a lot of fun but it requires that everyone be able to see what I'm doing here on this low table, so please gather around so you can see.

Activity
Dye in the Milk

Preparation: You'll need about 1/2 cup of 2% low fat milk, a few toothpicks, food coloring, dish soap, and a pie plate.

Pour about 1/4″ of 2% milk in the bottom of a pie plate. Put three drops of food coloring in one place onto the milk. Put three more drops of food coloring in another place on the milk. It's best to stick with primary colors (blue, red, and yellow) otherwise as they mix they end up turning brown or grey. Pause for a moment and say, "This milk is like our hearts and these drops are like things that we end of believing or doing that aren't the best. We need to be corrected.

Using a toothpick place a drop of liquid detergent into the center of the dye. Continue putting drops of detergent at different places in the milk and dye and watch the dye swirl around in the milk. The chemical reaction between the fat in the milk and the detergent creates an interesting show. Then say to the children, "Sometimes kids don't like to be corrected. Many adults have a hard time with

correction. But if you learn to receive correction some great things can happen. In this case even the mistakes or wrong things that are done can turn into something nice. Correction is valuable because it helps us learn and grow.

● ● ● ● ●

Transition

We're now going to play a game. We have set up an obstacle course made of chairs. The person has to walk through the whole obstacle course without touching any of the chairs to get to the other side. The hard part is that you will be blindfolded and you'll have a guide helping you get through the course. The guide will use correction to help you if you start moving in the wrong way.

Activity
Obstacle Course

Preparation: You'll need a blindfold. Set up an obstacle course with chairs.

Choose one person to be blindfolded. This person must walk through an obstacle course of chairs without bumping into any of them. After blindfolding the first volunteer, choose another person to be the guide. Say something like, "You two are working as a team to get the blindfolded person through the obstacle course and to the treasure on the other side. What can we pretend are some of the pitfalls waiting to get the person?" Let people imagine sinking sand pits, wild animals, steep cliffs, and other dangers. The guide must lead the person through the obstacle course. Have a camera ready to take a picture for your photo diary.

For older children, you may even move the chairs around after the child is blindfolded. This is a fun game but it requires that each person listen to the correction of the other person in order to get through the whole obstacle course without touching any of the chairs. Correction is valuable because it helps us learn and grow.

Young children can guide the person using their hands and their voices. Older children might only use their voices to guide the person through.

You may also have several teams working at the same time to accomplish the goal.

During this activity the teacher can say things like, "I see guides correcting. That's good. We all need correction at times." And "Without correction, your person might fall over a cliff or get into trouble." Look for ways to talk about correction in a positive sense and look for examples of the value of correction to share later.

● ● ● ● ●

Transition

Correction helps us in a lot of ways. Often we don't even realize it. Sometimes parents correct their kids to help them because they see something that the child doesn't see. Unfortunately, kids may react to correction and don't see how valuable it really is. We're going to have a snack now that illustrates the hidden benefits of correction. Correction is like buried treasure. These cookies and candies have treasure buried inside.

Snack Idea
Treasure Cookies

Preparation: Provide cookies or treats with hidden filling, cream, or chocolate inside. You may also want to obtain some candy with surprise centers and give each child one or two pieces.

Talk about how correction has hidden benefits inside.

Ask children how they have grown or learned something through correction. Children may focus on sports, math, or other skills. Ask kids, "Since we learn and grow from correction, why do we not like it?"

Transition

We're going to play another game to illustrate the value of correction. It's called the Treasure Detector Game. I'm going to need all of your help to make this game work. It's a game that uses correction to help a child find a treasure. Remember, correction is valuable because it helps us learn and grow.

Game
Treasure Detector Game

Preparation: Provide a beanbag.

Have children sit in a circle. Use a beanbag as a treasure and tell children that when the beanbag gets close to them they should beep because they are the treasure detectors. You might explain a little more about a metal detector that makes a beeping noise as it gets close to metal. In fact, people use metal detectors to discover treasure even today.

To demonstrate, practice moving the beanbag around the room and as you get closer to particular children then have them beep louder and louder. After the children have the idea of what a metal detector does they're ready to play the game.

Choose one child to volunteer to go out of the room. Give the beanbag to another child who will sit on it. All children should appear to be sitting on the beanbag and not give away where the real treasure is. When the volunteer Treasure Hunter comes back into the room, all the children should beep quietly as he moves into the circle. As he gets closer to the "treasure" the children should beep more loudly until the Treasure Hunter picks the right person and discovers the treasure.

When this game is played right, the Treasure Hunter gets close to the child, hears the increase noise, and then goes past the child to test their guess. If the noise decreases when he/she moves past and then increases again when close, then the child has used correction to make the right choice. This game requires that children listen to others and learn from them in order to make the right guess.

Allow the person who held the treasure to be the next Treasure Hunter and continue the game for several turns. You can vary the game by placing the treasure somewhere else in the room in order to guide the Treasure Hunter to the right place.

At the end of the game ask the question, "What does this game teach about correction?" Discuss ways that correction helps us reach our goals in life. If you're going down the wrong path without correction, you'll just get lost. We need to respond to correction in life in order to get to our goal most successfully.

Activity
Correction Color Page

Preparation: Photocopy the color page at the end of this lesson. Provide markers or crayons.

Allow children to color the page while you talk about correction and its value both in the family and elsewhere in life.

Review and Close

Come together for a group time and talk again about the value of correction. Discuss how we grow treasure in our hearts when we learn to accept correction from others. Have a few students share about times they were corrected and what they learned from the experience. End by challenging the children to see correction as a treasure. Pray for the students before they leave.

Treasure Chest

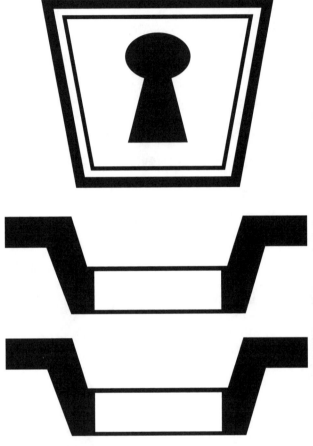

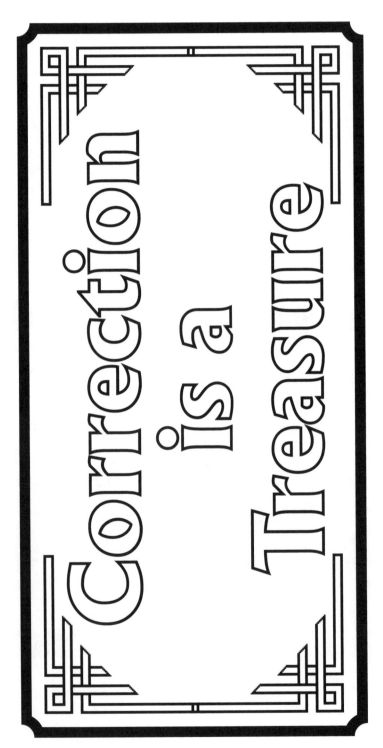

Correction is a Treasure

The Wise Donkey Craft

Glue the donkey's tongue (below) underneath the flap of the bag.

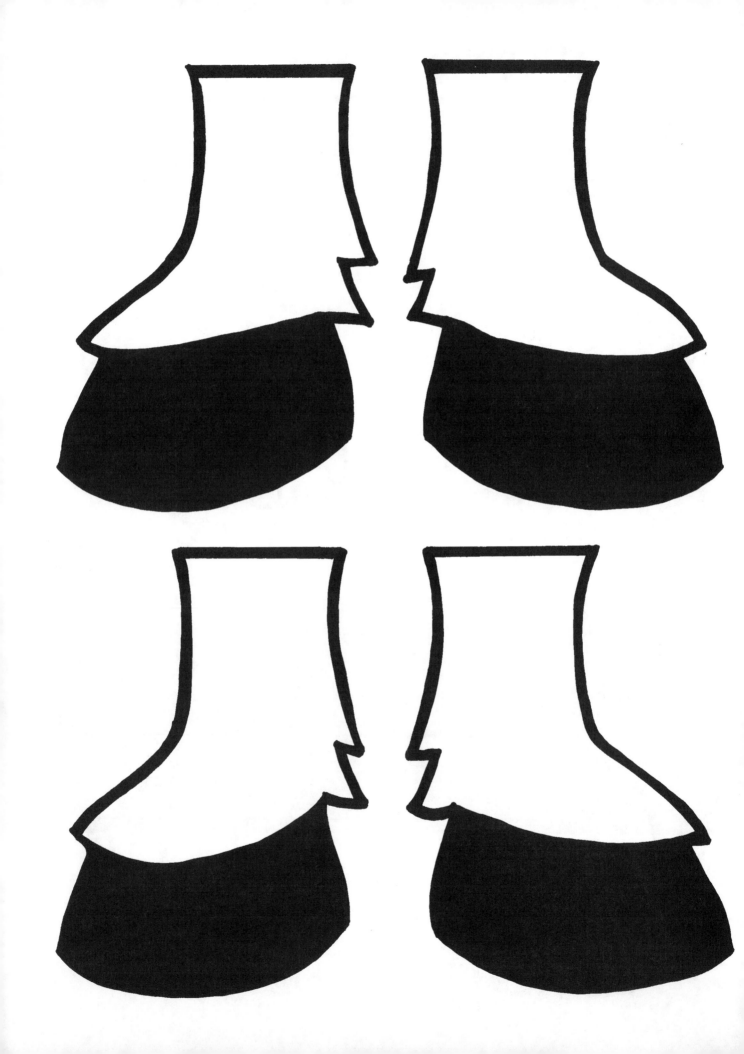

Correction is a Treasure

"For these commands are a lamp, this teaching is a light, and the corrections of discipline are the way to life." *Proverbs 6:23*

76 Hopatcong Drive, Lawrenceville, NJ 08648-4136
(800) 771-8334 or (609) 771-8002
Email: parent@biblicalparenting.org
Web: biblicalparenting.org

Listen to the Donkey

Dear Parent,

Children often view correction as an attack and then defend themselves at all costs. In this lesson your child learned that correction is a valuable tool for heart change. Through the Bible story of Balaam and the Donkey in Numbers 22, children saw the importance of listening to others even when you can't understand why, or you don't agree.

Theme: Correction is valuable because it helps me learn and grow.

Through activities and games children learned the value of correction. Each of the activities emphasized the importance of making adjustments in our lives in order to grow and be strong. In short, correction is a gift. You might ask your child about making a paper airplane or about the milk experiment that demonstrated how the heart changes in special ways.

Teaching children to value correction is not an easy task. We're sure you wish your child would consider correction valuable, but instead your attempts are met with resistance. Keep in mind that heart change usually takes quite a bit longer than mere behavior adjustment. Look for ways to remind your child about the value of correction.

The Bible verse for this lesson is especially helpful. You may want to put it up on the wall in your home. It's Proverbs 6:23 "For these commands are a lamp, this teaching is a light, and the corrections of discipline are the way to life."

By the way, how do you handle correction? This isn't just a child problem is it? As adults we must value correction and see it as a way to learn and grow. Share your own thoughts about correction with your child. That can lead to an interesting and helpful discussion.

Blessings,

Scott Turansky   Joanne Miller
National Center for Biblical Parenting
www.biblicalparenting.org

When Children Believe "It's Not My Fault"

Preparing Your Heart to Teach Session 5

How do you respond when you make a mistake? People do different things when they discover an error on their part. Some people get angry, others blame, and some people plague themselves with guilt.

One of the signs of maturity for children or adults is learning how to handle mistakes. We've all heard that we can learn from mistakes, and that's certainly important, but how do we treat ourselves? If we spend a lot of time regretting or punishing ourselves then we end up robbing ourselves of joy in life.

Two responses tend to dominate most people as they face their own mistakes. First, some people do a lot of blaming. After all, my mistakes are often caused by a number of factors, and I can usually emphasize those factors that are other people's fault. Blamers experience a lot of anger and feel like victims much of the time because everyone else is in control of their wellbeing.

A second response is to attack yourself with self-condemnation. "I'm stupid. I'll never get it right." These kinds of statements lead to feelings of inadequacy and unworthiness. People who engage in self-condemnation limit themselves, refuse to try new things lest they fail again, and generally have a weak view of their capabilities.

A better response is to learn to accept responsibility for one's part of the problem, learn from the mistake, and go on to try again. In fact, a healthy form of self-correction goes through a process of admitting a mistake, understanding why it was a mistake, determining a better response, and giving yourself the freedom to try again.

What Children Learn in Session 5

Children must learn how to take responsibility for their mistakes and offenses. Two immature responses are targeted in this lesson. First, blaming is inappropriate and doesn't move a person forward in life. Secondly, kids who punish themselves for mistakes limit their ability to move on. Instead, in this lesson, children are taught to admit what they did wrong, determine why it was wrong, identify a different response next time, and are encouraged to try again.

Theme: When I'm wrong, I'll admit it.

Games, activities, and a Bible story contribute to this idea of responding well to mistakes. Being able to admit when you've done something wrong is a sign of maturity. But many children can't do that. In this lesson children will learn how to be humble and then take responsibility for their own mistakes.

Read Along in the Book, "Parenting is Heart Work"

Chapters 1 and 2 define the heart in practical ways. Understanding how the word "heart" is used in the scriptures, enables one to target discipline toward the heart. Chapter 16 gives specific strategies for using a Positive Conclusion and discusses why it works as a heart tool. Confession and humility are key ingredients necessary for addressing offenses or mistakes completely. Not only does the Positive Conclusion help address the subject of repentance in children, but it also forms the basis for a mature apology. Instead of just having kids say "sorry" to one another, children learn how to apologize in a way that addresses the offense and moves on.

Session 5

Theme

When I'm wrong, I'll admit it.

Welcome Activity
Create an Old Treasure Map

Preparation: In advance brew enough tea bags for each child to have one, eight tea bags per mug. Photocopy onto regular copy paper (20# bond) the first Treasure Map at the end of this lesson. Be prepared with a hair dryer and paper towels.

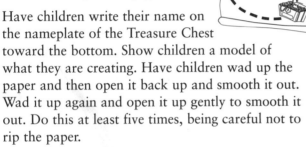

Have children write their name on the nameplate of the Treasure Chest toward the bottom. Show children a model of what they are creating. Have children wad up the paper and then open it back up and smooth it out. Wad it up again and open it up gently to smooth it out. Do this at least five times, being careful not to rip the paper.

Lay the paper out smooth on a plastic table or tablecloth. Pour some of the strong tea into a paper plate and give each child one of the tea bags. Caution the children to use the tea bags to dab, but not rub, the tea all over the paper. It's best to thoroughly soak the paper in tea both front and back. Be careful that the children don't work with the paper too long because it will begin to tear. Take pictures for your photo diary.

Take the soaked paper and place it on a paper towel. Use a hair dryer to thoroughly dry the paper. Set it aside for children to take home.

Take time to talk about the theme, "When I'm wrong, I'll admit it." In our lesson today we'll be learning about taking responsibility for our mistakes. That's an important part of correction. Instead of blaming others or looking for excuses, the best thing to do is to just admit when you've done something wrong. It's the fastest way to learn and grow.

Together Time

Use the ideas below along with your own thoughts and the Bible to dialogue with the children and help them see that it takes a mature person to admit when he's done the wrong thing.

Object Lesson
Shadow Lessons

Preparation: Bring a flashlight and a six inch tall action figure.

Dim or turn off the lights in the room. Place a six inch tall action figure on the table. Hold a flashlight about two feet above the figure creating just a small shadow. Continue to shine the flashlight on the little figure as you move the flashlight to increase the shadow's length. Ask children, "What can we learn about a light from a shadow?" Yes, we can learn where the light is. "When is a shadow longer, in the middle of the day or at the end of the day? Why?" A very interesting thing is going to happen in our story today and it has to do with a shadow.

Bible Story
Hezekiah and the Big Boo Boo

Hezekiah was a king—a good king. In fact, he was one of the best kings that Judah ever had, but he made a big mistake and needed to be corrected. Even good people need to experience correction sometimes, even kings. Let me tell you the story.

Hezekiah got very sick. He wasn't being punished. In fact, I don't think he did anything wrong that led to his sickness. It started with a boil that just got worse and worse. They didn't have doctors in those days and a small sore, if not treated, could get so bad that a person could die. Hezekiah knew that, and he didn't know what else to do. *Will I recover? I've got an idea! I'll call the prophet Isaiah. He'll tell me the truth. After all, I've served the Lord all my life. I don't think God is done with me yet.*

Hezekiah had done a lot of things for God. He was a man of action, reestablishing the priestly duties and getting the temple functioning again. The people were worshiping God just the way God wanted. Hezekiah worked hard to get rid of idolatry in Israel, and he accomplished a lot during his reign of only fifteen years. But he had so much yet to do. He wasn't ready to die. Was this the end of his life? He felt like it; he was so sick.

The king's officials sent a message to the prophet Isaiah, who paid a visit to the king. Hezekiah waited as Isaiah talked to the Lord to see what God would do. After a little while Isaiah turned to the king to give him the message. "God says you will not recover. You had better put your house in order. You're going to die."

Hezekiah couldn't believe what he heard. As Isaiah walked out his bedroom door, the king just stared. Could it be true? And then Hezekiah began to cry. As the tears came, he turned his face to the wall and prayed, "Lord, I've served you all these years with my whole heart. Please remember how I've walked with you and heal me. I don't want to die."

A knock on the door interrupted Hezekiah's prayer. "Come in." It was Isaiah.

"Yes?" the king said.

"Before I even left your palace, God gave me another message."

"Well, what is it?"

"He told me that he's heard your prayer and has seen your tears, and he will heal you. You'll get well in the next three days."

Oh, that is so great! Thank you, Lord. Hezekiah was so happy. One minute he was crying because he was so sad and the next minute he was happy. He would get well. He would be able to help his country more. Hezekiah was so grateful that God would let him live a little longer.

Hezekiah still felt sick though. He wanted to make sure that Isaiah was telling him the truth. "Isaiah, can you give me a sign that this will actually take place?"

Isaiah thought for a moment. "Yes. In fact, you can choose. See the shadow on the long staircase over there? The sun is setting and the shadow is going down the stairs one at a time. Would you like the shadow to jump ten stairs ahead or ten stairs back?"

Now boys and girls how could a shadow jump ten stairs one way or the other? The sun would have to move to a different place in the sky. Can the sun just jump from here to there? No, it can't. This was an amazing question because Isaiah was saying that God was about to do a miracle just for Hezekiah. Which would you choose, having the sun go ahead or back ten stairs on the staircase? Why?

Hezekiah thought for a moment. "Well, the normal thing is for the sun to go ahead, so I'd like to see the sun go back ten stairs."

"O God of heaven, please reveal yourself to King Hezekiah by moving the shadow back."

Hezekiah's eyes grew wide as he watched! The shadow went back. God did a special miracle just for Hezekiah. *Whoa! That's really something. I just choose and God does it. That is amazing power.*

During the next three days the king improved. The boil went down. He felt better, and could tell he was getting well. He kept thinking about that sign. *I can't believe it. I got to tell God what to do, and he did it.* Pride began to grow in Hezekiah's heart.

A short time later a group of men came to Jerusalem. Guards came to Hezekiah to report the good news. "The king of Babylon heard you were sick and wanted to wish you well, so he sent these messengers."

"Send them in! They can see that I'm well. In fact, I'll take them on a tour of the palace and show them around."

So Hezekiah gave the group from Babylon a personal tour. He showed them room after room of treasures. Hezekiah enjoyed watching their mouths drop open as he opened each door. In fact, the king showed his guests everything, even his armory and all the weapons he'd stored up.

Hezekiah didn't realize it, but his pride was getting him further and further into trouble. These men weren't really friends. They were the enemy. They would come someday and rob King Hezekiah. The king didn't realize it but his pride was causing him to give away secrets that no one should know.

The guests said, "You have done a great job as king. You have so much. Your God must be pleased with you. In fact, we even heard that a miraculous sign happened right here in Jerusalem. Can you tell us about it?"

"Oh yes, you're right. God is pleased with me." Hezekiah smiled. "The sign happened just the other day. I got to tell God what to do. He asked me whether I wanted to have the shadow go back or forward ten steps on that staircase over there. I said 'back,' and that's what he did."

Hezekiah enjoyed telling his guests about all his accomplishments and the miraculous sign. As they were leaving, Isaiah came back into the palace. Hezekiah was about to realize the danger he was in. "Who were those guys?"

"A special group of men from Babylon to wish me well."

"What did you tell them?"

"I showed them all around the palace."

"Oh no. You didn't."

"Yes I did. Why?"

"You didn't show them all the storehouses and the armory, did you?"

"Yes, but you don't have to worry, Isaiah. They're from hundreds of miles away."

"You are the one who doesn't understand, O King. A time will come when armies from Babylon will conquer Jerusalem and take away all these riches."

At that moment, Hezekiah realized the pride that was in his heart. *How could I have been so foolish? I was thinking how great I am when I should have been talking about how great God is. I can't believe I did that. I exposed my entire kingdom to danger.*

The king did a very important thing just then. He could have said, "It's not my fault. They tricked me." Or, "Why didn't someone warn me?" Hezekiah could have blamed his problem on someone else or complained that it wasn't his fault. He didn't do that. Instead, the Bible tells us what the king did. In fact, this one thing that Hezekiah did shows us that he was a pretty mature man. The Bible tells us that the king repented. He was sorry for boasting about himself instead of giving God the credit. He just apologized.

Isaiah said, "Because you have responded well to correction, God says he won't allow this judgment to come on Jerusalem during your lifetime."

Hezekiah realized he'd allowed his heart to grow proud. He was grateful for the prophet who corrected him so he could make a change in his heart before he did further damage. Hezekiah realized how valuable correction was because it prevented a terrible thing from happening. The king repented instead of arguing. Because he responded well, God didn't bring the judgment on him.

For Younger Children

This Bible story is rather complicated so for younger children you may want to emphasize the fact that King Hezekiah was proud, boasting about all he had and didn't

realize the danger he was in. When the prophet Isaiah corrected him he responded well. Children can also respond well to correction.

This story was taken from 2 Kings 20:1–21, Isaiah 39:1–8, and 2 Chronicles 32:26.

Bible Verse

Psalm 32:5
"I will confess my transgressions to the Lord and you forgave the guilt of my sin."

For younger children: "I will confess my sin."

Transition

One of the problems with blaming is that it divides people. Instead of everyone doing their part, people become selfish trying to protect something. Then the teamwork idea falls apart. People become more interested in blaming others than getting anything done. We're going to play a game together that you'll like.

Game
Cotton Ball Air Hockey

Preparation: You'll need masking tape, three cotton balls for each child, and flexible drinking straws.

Using masking tape, divide a table into sections. With four people divide the table into four parts, with eight people, use the tape to make a grid with eight sections, one for each person sitting around the table.

Place three cotton balls in each section and a flexible drinking straw. "Please sit down at the table and don't touch anything. In a moment I'm going to have you pick up the drinking straw. Instead of blowing in the short end of the drinking straw you will blow into the long end allowing you to aim the shorter end at the cotton balls.

Everyone has three cotton balls in front of them. When I say go, you will blow the cotton balls to other grids in the table trying to keep your square

empty. You may stand up but you may not get on the table. You may only use your hands to stop cotton balls from going off the table or to pick them up from the floor if they fall. Are you ready? Go."

Typically, many cotton balls land on the floor and kids have fun trying to blow them back and forth. Stop the game after about a minute or so and say, "That was fun but we just had a lot of cotton balls falling on the ground and people blowing them at each other. Everyone was working against everyone else. Now, we're going to change the game a bit."

Put a placemat in the center of the table or tape down a piece of 11x17 paper. "The goal now is to have everyone work together to blow the cotton balls onto the placemat. The same rules apply. You can't touch the cotton balls unless they fall off the table and you can use your hands to stop them from falling off. Are you ready? Go."

Typically, children blow toward the placemat, sometimes blowing the cotton balls off the other side. It's a challenge to get the cotton balls onto the placemat. Whether all the cotton balls make it on or not, you can say something like, "What's the difference between the two games?" One focuses on trying to blow the cotton balls toward another person. That makes them opponents. The other has kids blowing together to accomplish a task. That makes them team members. Sometimes people were giving instructions or even correcting others. That's part of working as a team. Every person is taking responsibility for his or her part.

Today we're talking about correcting. When you accept correction well you learn quickly and there's a sense of cooperation instead of competition.

Transition

One of the ways that we all learn how to do things better is to stop and ask ourselves some questions. We have a craft that helps us know what questions to ask. Whenever anything goes wrong, whether you make a mistake, or you disobey, or you have

a bad attitude, you can ask these questions: "What did I do wrong?" "Why was that wrong?" "What am I going to do differently next time?" And then say to yourself, "Okay, I'll go ahead and try again."

Craft
Find the Treasures to Make a Map

Preparation: Photocopy onto cardstock the numbered boxes and the map at the end of this lesson. Cut out the boxes and place all clue #1 into one envelope, #2 into another, and so on. Before children arrive take the four envelopes and hide them in the room as instructed. Have glue and crayons or markers ready.

This is an activity and a craft. Have children color the road and decorate their page. Then say something like, "We have four things missing on the page. Each missing piece is marked by a dotted line and a number. The first missing square for everyone is in an envelope hidden in this room. You are all Treasure Hunters. I'm going to give you a clue and you are going to go find the envelope. When you find it, you may take one piece out of the envelope and bring it back to your table and glue that piece on your map."

Have the four envelopes placed in strategic places around the room. The following ideas give you a way to play this in one classroom. However, if you have an extended play area you might use your imagination to increase the fun. You might have kids glue on their treasure after each clue or have them find all the treasures before gluing all four onto their paper. Keep the age of the child in mind as you develop the difficulty of the clues.

You might put one taped under a table with the clue, "This part of the treasure is in an envelope that you can only see when you are down very low." A second envelope could be in a leader's pocket with the clue, "This part of the treasure is

revealed when you say the magic words to the right person. The magic words are, 'I really really like you. What do you think of me?' Most leaders would reply, 'I really really really like you but I don't have the treasure.' The right leader says, "I really really really like you and I have something for you." A third envelope might be hidden under a box of tissues on a counter and the clue could read, "If you cry a lot you'll discover this part of the treasure." The last part of the treasure might be behind a curtain and the clue might be, "This envelope is hidden behind something."

Take time to have children glue the right box onto their Treasure Map. Then talk about the map. This is a map that helps us know how to handle mistakes that we make in life. We ask three questions and then make a statement. Allow one of the children to pretend to be Hezekiah from the story. Ask the three questions and a statement and see if the child can respond.

For Younger Children

Place the clues in obvious places where a child can easily find them. Choose one child from the group and say, "The first clue is in an envelope on the counter." Or "The second clue is in my pocket."

● ● ● ● ●

Transition

The three questions and a statement are very important. They help us know how to learn from mistakes. Some kids blame other people when they make mistakes or they blame themselves and say, "I'm never going to get it right." In this next activity we're going to practice asking these questions and you're going to help me.

Role Play
The Hovering Ping Pong Ball

Preparation: Bring a vacuum cleaner into class that has a hose and set the machine to blow air out. Also have a ping-pong ball ready.

When you place a ping-pong ball about 12" from the nozzle then hold the nozzle pointing straight

up, the blowing air keeps the ball in place instead of blowing it away.

Tell children that you know that a ping-pong ball will hover if you turn on the air. So here's how it works. Instead of putting the ball 12″ away, put the ball right on the nozzle and let it go. Of course, it blows right into the room. "Oops I did something wrong. Help me with the three questions and a statement. What did I do wrong? etc." Some children will not go through the questions but instead will want to tell you what to do differently next time. Stop and force them to think of what you did wrong first. Try a couple of times unsuccessfully to hover the ball and ask children to help you answer the questions. This is an excellent way to model learning from mistakes using the three questions and a statement. Finally do it right and enjoy the children's response. Have a camera ready to take a picture for your photo diary.

● ● ● ● ● ————————

Transition

Correction is an important part of life. We often learn by making mistakes. Unfortunately, some kids yell at themselves or put themselves down when they make a mistake. Others blame the people around them. The best way to handle a mistake is to admit it. You can ask the three questions and make the statement on your Treasure Map. We call that the Positive Conclusion.

Here's another way to look at the same three questions and a statement. Hold up the model of the bookmark you've created. These are in the shape of stairs to remind you of the story of Hezekiah and the shadow on the stairs. These three questions and a statement are so important we wanted to give you something to remind you about them. This is an example of a bookmark that you will be able to take home today. We're going to cut it out and put yarn in it now.

Craft (For Older Children) Bookmark

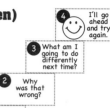

Preparation: Photocopy the bookmark page at the back of this lesson providing one bookmark for every child. You'll also need a hole punch and yarn.

Using a hole-punch, create a hole where designated. Allow children to cut out their bookmark and put yarn through the hole. Three pieces of yarn allow children to braid it nicely. You may choose to teach children how to braid. Be sure to use the Positive Conclusion to model how we learn from mistakes.

Take time to talk about how valuable the three questions and a statement are for solving problems and learning from mistakes. You might even correct a child who makes a mistake in class and say, "I'm going to correct Billy. Let's see how he responds to the three questions and a statement."

● ● ● ● ● ————————

Transition

We all learn from making mistakes. At least I hope you do. I guess some people keep making the same mistakes over and over again. If we learn from mistakes we grow and get better. In this next game you'll have to fail in order to win. Let's see how you learn from your mistakes.

Game (For Younger Children) Find the Path to the Treasure

Preparation: Lay a bed sheet on the floor and create a grid with masking tape. Make 16 squares, four rows of four, as large as the bed sheet will allow. Take 20 pieces of opaque paper and put a large "X" on eight of them. (This gives you 12 blank and 8 with X's so you have some choices.)

Start by placing the X's on the squares face up to form a path from one corner to the other. You don't have to use all eight. Talk to children about the path of X's that lead to the treasure. Then, as children watch, move the X's to a different pattern showing a different path to the treasure. When you think children have the general idea, turn the pages upside down and add the blank pages all around so that every square is filled with a page. Thus the path to the treasure is hidden.

Choose one Treasure Hunter to start at the beginning by standing at one corner where the first X is located. In order to take a step, the child must choose a square. Turn the paper over and if it contains an X, he can move forward. Each time he chooses a blank piece of paper, stop and see where the progress is already and then turn all the pieces upside down again. Allow the child to learn by first trying to remember where the X's were last time and then trying a new way to the finish.

Game (For Older Children)
Find the Path to the Treasure

Preparation:

Photocopy onto heavy cardstock the 36-square game board at the end of this lesson. Also photocopy the playing piece page onto cardstock so that children can't see through the game pieces. You may want to cut out the playing pieces in advance for the children so that they can just play the game. Provide envelopes to keep the game pieces in.

Children pair up for this game. One is the player and the other is the coach. The player goes out of the room while the coach places the game pieces upside down on the board. First, the coach creates a path of "X" pieces from the start to the treasure. Squares are considered "touching" when they

share an edge or a corner. Then the coach places blank cards upside down on the remaining squares. When the player returns, all the game pieces look the same and the path is hidden.

The player starts her turn by taking a first step, turning over one game piece in the starting corner. Then she has three choices. If she chooses the right one, an X, then she's on the right path and moves again. She continues to move forward toward the treasure until she accidentally turns up a blank square When a blank appears, the coach asks, "What did you do wrong?" The player answers, "I went here." The coach asks, "Why was that wrong?" The player answers, "Because it was a blank." The coach asks, "What are you going to do differently?" The player says, "I'm going to go here." The coach says, "Okay, go ahead and try again." The player turns all the pieces back upside down and starts all over. The only way to win is to get through the whole path without hitting a blank square.

Some children take a while to learn and even make the same mistake over and over. The coach must be patient and just go through the questions and a statement, and not give any hints. When the first child is successful, if you have enough time, the player becomes the coach and sets the board up for the new player.

This game is excellent for children who tend to get angry with themselves for making a mistake. It teaches them a better way to respond to mistakes instead of self-condemnation.

● ● ● ● ●

Transition

Even the greatest scientists make mistakes. In fact, people learn from mistakes and often create some great things. Sometimes when we make mistakes, the error still turns out okay. In part, it has to do with the way we think about the mistakes we make. In our snack today I made some cookies. These cookies were a mistake when the very first person made them. Now many people like them. I'm interested to know what you think.

Snack
Mistake Cookies

Preparation: Bake or buy chocolate chip cookies.

Serve children chocolate chip cookies. If you get ambitious or you want to be creative, bake your own cookies. Make one batch by melting the chocolate and mixing it into the other ingredients. This makes chocolate cookies. In the other batch, make regular chocolate chip cookies, or break up a chocolate bar so that the chips look obviously different. You can tell, or read to children the following story:

Ruth Wakefield was an innkeeper in the 1930's. She was baking a batch of her favorite cookies called Butter Drop Do cookies using a recipe that was quite old, back to the colonial times. She decided she wanted chocolate cookies this time so she cut up a Nestlé chocolate bar and put chunks into the batter. She expected that the chocolate would mix right into the batter as it all heated up. But she made a mistake. Her idea didn't work. Instead, she ended up with butter cookies with chunks of chocolate in them. Her mistake turned into one of the most favorite cookies of all time: chocolate chip cookies.

● ● ● ● ●

Transition

Blaming means you point your finger at someone else instead of yourself. Everyone point at someone else for a moment. Now freeze. Look at your fingers. Usually when you point at someone else, three fingers are pointing back at you. That's a good reminder when we start blaming. We shouldn't be too quick to point our finger at other people. We should remember to look at ourselves first.

Craft
Pointing Finger

Preparation:
Photocopy the hand at the end of this lesson onto heavy cardstock. Provide pieces of yarn for each child about 10″ long.

Ask children, "If you have an important thing you want to remember and you think you might forget, what kind of things do you do to remind yourself?" Children might write it down, put up a note, ask Mom to help, or even set an alarm. Tell children, "One idea some people used to use is that they would tie a string around their finger until they did the job. So we're going to tie a string around this cardboard finger and then you can put this up on your wall or somewhere to remind you to be careful not to blame others, but instead, look at the three fingers pointing back at you. We all need to take responsibility for our part of the problem.

The kids will cut out the finger and tie a piece of yarn on it. The idea is to turn blaming (pointing the finger at someone else) to remembering (pointing the finger up with yarn on it) to remember to take responsibility for your own mistakes.

For Younger Children
You'll want to cut out the hands in advance and you'll have to tie the yarn on the finger for them as well.

Session 5

Review and Close

Who can tell me what someone should do if they make a mistake? Children may explore answers like, "Say you're sorry," "fix the problem," "tell your mom what you did." All of these are good answers and you can use this opportunity to talk about forgiveness, confession, and the negative effects of lying and hiding a mistake. Reinforce the ideas from this lesson: When I'm wrong, I'll admit it.

Boys and girls, let me tell you a story. Dave was eight years old. He was being silly and he accidentally broke a light on the outside of his neighbor's house. Later that day the broken light was discovered. Dave said that Richie, another neighbor, broke it. Dave lied. That night, Dave was in bed and he started feeling terrible. He knew that he had done two wrong things. Can anyone tell me what the two wrong things were? Yes, he was silly and accidentally broke the light, but then he did something else wrong: he lied. Dave felt bad in his heart. He knew that other people might not find out what he had done, but *he* knew and God also knew what really happened.

Dave decided to get up out of bed and tell his mom the truth. Mom listened to what Dave said and then said, "I'm so glad you have a conscience that won't let you go to sleep if you do the wrong thing. That's a sign of maturity and a sign that you are strong on the inside. I'm so grateful. Let's talk about what happened. What did you do wrong?"
"I broke the light and then lied about it."
"Why was that wrong?"
"I shouldn't have been silly like that and then telling a lie is not being honest."
"What are you going to do differently next time?"
"Well first, I won't be silly like that at the neighbors house. And if I do break something I'll tell the truth and admit it instead of trying to cover it up."
"That's good, Dave. Okay, you can go now, but I think you have one more thing to do before you can have a clear conscience about this. Do you know what that is?"
"Yes, I should pray and ask God to forgive me for lying and then I should tell our neighbor too."
"Yes, you're right. Tomorrow we'll go talk to the neighbor and see how we can make it right, okay?"

Dave went back up to bed and he felt much better in his heart. Why do you think he felt better? Because he admitted what he did wrong. He went through the three questions and a statement and he determined to make it right with the neighbor.

We all need to recognize that a Positive Conclusion like that is a treasure in our lives. It helps us gain a clear conscience and it helps us think rightly about the mistakes and offenses we have in life.

TREASURE MAP

You are here

Find the Treasures to Make a Map
Game Pieces

1 What did I do wrong?	**1** What did I do wrong?	**1** What did I do wrong?	**1** What did I do wrong?
2 Why was that wrong?	**2** Why was that wrong?	**2** Why was that wrong?	**2** Why was that wrong?
3 What am I going to do differently next time?	**3** What am I going to do differently next time?	**3** What am I going to do differently next time?	**3** What am I going to do differently next time?
4 I'll go ahead and try again.	**4** I'll go ahead and try again.	**4** I'll go ahead and try again.	**4** I'll go ahead and try again.

Session 5

Bookmark

4 I'll go ahead and try again.

3 What am I going to do differently next time?

2 Why was that wrong?

4 I'll go ahead and try again.

1 What did I do wrong?

3 What am I going to do differently next time?

4 I'll go ahead and try again.

2 Why was that wrong?

1 What did I do wrong?

3 What am I going to do differently next time?

2 Why was that wrong?

1 What did I do wrong?

START

FINISH

Session 5

Find the Path to the Treasure
Game Pieces

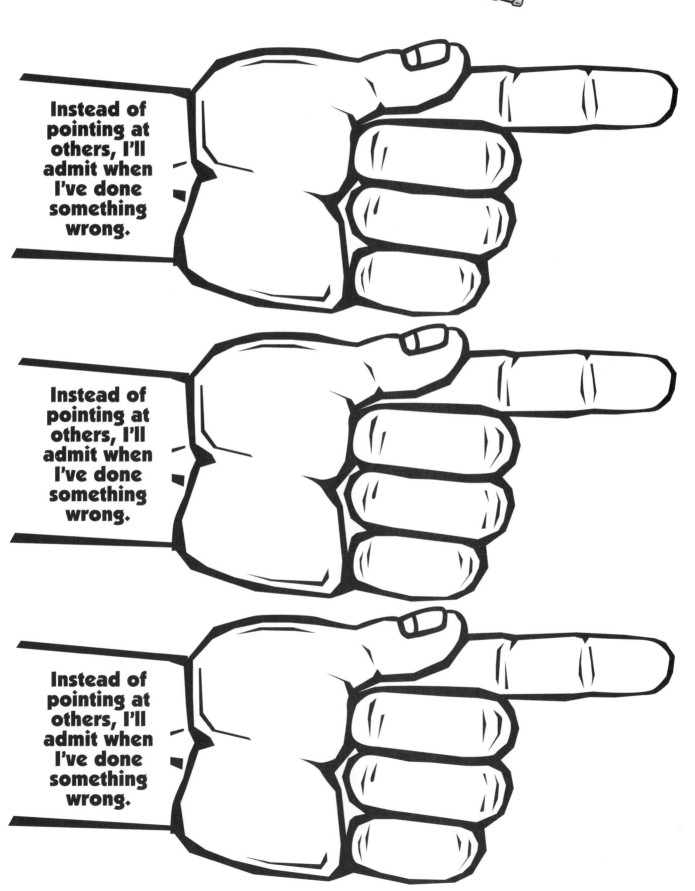

 76 Hopatcong Drive, Lawrenceville, NJ 08648-4136
(800) 771-8334 or (609) 771-8002
Email: parent@biblicalparenting.org
Web: biblicalparenting.org

When You're Wrong, Admit It

Dear Parent,

Some children have quite a problem with blaming others when they're corrected. Other children blame themselves and beat themselves up over their mistakes. Both of these problems were addressed in this week's lesson. Children learned how to process mistakes and offenses by taking responsibility for their own part of the problem.

Theme: When I'm wrong, I'll admit it.

Children sometimes view admission of wrong-doing as a sign of weakness. In this lesson we emphasized the importance of taking personal responsibility and then moving on with some solutions. We encouraged children to ask themselves three questions and then make one statement. They are:

> What did I do wrong?
> Why was that wrong?
> What am I going to do differently next time?
> Go ahead and try again.

This isn't just a kid solution; it's also a healthy way for adults to think about mistakes. In this lesson we taught children that when they can follow these steps, they'll grow faster and become wiser. The Bible story was about Hezekiah, taken from 2 Kings 20:1–21, Isaiah 39:1–8, and 2 Chronicles 32:26. You might want to read that story to your child and discuss the way Hezekiah responded to his mistake.

Here are some questions you might ask your child about this lesson: What are *Mistake Cookies?* Why does that cardboard finger you brought home have a string tied on it? How should you respond when you make a mistake?

The Bible verse we talked about is "I will confess my transgressions to the Lord and you forgave the guilt of my sin." Psalm 32:5

Important lessons are often learned from mistakes but in order to grow and move forward you have to be able to respond well to those mistakes. If children can learn this truth early, they'll be much more successful as they get older.

Blessings,

Scott Turansky   Joanne Miller
National Center for Biblical Parenting
www.biblicalparenting.org

What to Do When the Answer is No

Preparing Your Heart to Teach Session 6

How are you doing at living within limits? We live in a society that encourages us to bypass boundaries and indulge ourselves. So many people eat more than is best and have a hard time with their weight. We're encouraged to spend more money than we have. Credit cards enable people to live on next month's income to pay for this month's lifestyle.

An important lesson we all must learn is to be content with what we have instead of longing for more and more and more. Advertisers spend billions of dollars trying to convince consumers that what we have is not good enough.

Learning to live within limits is essential for a healthy and enjoyable life. The word "no" then becomes a helpful restraint. When we say "no" to our desires we learn to be satisfied with what we have instead of complaining about what we don't have. One wise counselor said, "Tell me what you need and I'll tell you how you can live without it." We often think we need things and then after we get them we change our minds.

Contentment is one of the keys to a joyful life. Paul said in Philippians 4:11-12 that he learned to be content. That's an encouragement to all of us. Contentment can be learned and as we accept the limits of life we grow in this area.

What Children Learn in Session 6

Kids don't like it when they get no as an answer. They often become unhappy and then mistreat Mom or Dad. People who can't live within limits are never happy. The solution is to learn contentment, the ability to live within limits and enjoy life within those boundaries. Children tend to resort to three manipulative techniques when they don't get what they want. They argue, badger, or whine. In this lesson children are confronted with those manipulations and receive a vision for a better way.

Theme: Accepting no as an answer shows maturity.

Using the story of Paul and Silas in prison, children learn that they can have a positive outlook even when things don't go their way. Games, activities, and a snack all help motivate kids to accept no as an answer.

Read Along in the Book, "Parenting is Heart Work"

Chapter 3 explores the will of a child. Some kids have strong wills and others lack motivation. All children fall somewhere on that continuum. One of the ways the will is revealed is when children can't have what they want. In these moments children often challenge their parents and look for ways to get around a no answer. The solution is a heart-based approach. Chapter 7 discusses the heart as the place where emotions reside and offers suggestions for addressing them. Grief is explained as the process of letting go. Understanding a child's emotions is a key to touching the heart.

Session 6

Theme

Accepting no as an answer shows maturity.

Welcome Activity
Arm Badge

Preparation: Photocopy the page for the arm badge at the end of this lesson. Also provide some file folders or other stiff cardboard. You'll also need crayons or markers, a hole punch, glue, and rubber bands.

I Can Accept No as an Answer!

Each child can cut out the arm badge and glue it onto the stiff cardboard. For younger children you'll want to cut out the cardboard and arm badges for them in advance. Punch holes in the two sides and fasten a rubber band to each side. Decorate the front with colored pens. Kids can slide the arm badge over their wrist or arm to remind themselves that they can accept no as an answer.

• • • • •

Together Time

Use the ideas below along with your own thoughts and the Bible to dialogue with the children and help them see that they can learn to accept no as an answer. It just means changing their perspective a bit.

Object Lesson
Tied up and Singing

Preparation: You'll need a piece of rope or a scarf.

Ask the children, "Who would like to come up and be my assistant? It has to be someone who can sing a song." Invite a volunteer to come up. Use a rope or scarf to tie up the child and ask him to sing while he's tied up. You might just tie the hands or if you think the volunteer can handle it, tie the child to a chair. If you don't get a volunteer

you might have to be the singing prisoner yourself or have someone accompany you to be tied up and sing. You might say, "It's hard to imagine being a prisoner and singing at the same time, right? Usually we think of singing as a happy activity. A person tied up is usually sad. It's not easy to put those two things together, is it? In our story today though we see exactly that thing.

Bible Story
The Singing Prisoners

Paul liked to travel and tell people about Jesus. Each place he went he told people about the Lord and some responded well; others didn't like it. So sometimes Paul was treated very well and other times people were mean to him.

One time Paul was on the Island of Malta. He told people about Jesus and he prayed for people who were sick and they got well. The chief official on the island, Publius, was very kind to Paul and he made sure that Paul and his friends had the things they needed. In fact, he fed them well and took care of them while they were there. How do you think Paul felt to eat good food?

Kids, what is your favorite meal? What do you like for dessert? I wonder if Paul had those kinds of things. I'm sure Publius treated Paul quite well giving him the best meals that he could. I'm sure that Paul was very happy to eat such fine food.

Another time Paul told people about Jesus in the town of Philippi. He went down by the river where people were hanging out, and one woman named Lydia gave her life to Jesus. Lydia was so pleased that she too took Paul and his friends home and cared for them. Paul was often treated well because he had a message about Jesus that helped people.

But some people in Philippi didn't like Paul. In fact, they didn't like the new message he was bringing to their town so they had Paul thrown in prison. When you're in jail you don't get treated as nicely as when you're a guest in someone's house, do you? In fact, what kind of food do you think he got to eat while he and his friend Silas were in prison? I don't know exactly what he ate but I'm

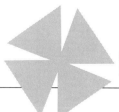

sure
it wasn't as good as
when he was a special guest.

A jailer was a man who was in charge of the prisoners. He was a very important man with a very important job. If the prisoners escaped while he was taking care of them, he would be punished. He might even get killed, so he was very careful to make sure that the prisoners did not escape. He put hand-cuffs on their hands and their feet and had them chained to the wall so they couldn't get away.

A very strong door also kept them in. There was no way to escape. It was dark and uncomfortable. How do you think Paul felt stuck in that prison? I would have thought he would feel sad because he was uncomfortable, or angry because he was mistreated.

But Paul did an amazing thing. He and his friend Silas began singing songs. Can you believe it? They were singing happy songs in the prison. They knew something very important. Joy doesn't come from things you have. It comes from your heart. Their hearts were happy even though they didn't have all kinds of nice food and they weren't even being treated very well.

What do you think the jailer would say if Paul would have asked for a hamburger? He would have said no. Do you think Paul would have gotten angry because the jailer said no? No, he just kept singing.

Sometimes when kids ask parents for things, parents say no. Some kids then get very angry. They start arguing, complaining, and even become mean with their parents just because they received a no answer.

What kinds of things does Mom or Dad say no to? Staying up later, going over to a friend's house, more time watching TV, or eating a snack right before dinner. The answer is sometimes no. When Mom or Dad says no, how do some kids respond? If you were angry with the no answer how might you respond?

Paul knew a very important lesson about life. Paul knew that things don't make people happy. It's what's inside the heart that's most important. Paul could sing in prison because his heart had joy in it. In fact, Paul wrote a letter a few years later to these same people in Philippi and he told them his secret. He said, "I have learned the secret of being content in any and every situation, whether well fed or hungry, whether living in plenty or in want. I can do everything through him who gives me strength."

Happiness is in your heart, not in external things. Paul knew that. He knew that Jesus could help him to be content in his heart even when things outside weren't the way he liked them.

The story of Paul in jail ends with a big earthquake. The ground shook and the chains came loose and the door of the prison came open. Paul was free. The jailer was now afraid because he knew that if his prisoners escaped he would be killed. He was very scared so Paul said, "We're all here." The jailer was so grateful that he brought Paul and Silas out and he took care of them and he gave them something to eat. I'm sure Paul and Silas were happy to eat again, but I'm also sure they were happy in their hearts because they knew that God was working.

The lesson from this story is an important one for all of us. Sometimes we don't get what we want. The answer is no. When that happens we have to decide how we're going to respond. Some people become angry and mistreat their parents just because they got a no answer. Paul says there's a secret that can help us accept a no answer. That secret has to do with our hearts and being content with what we have instead of complaining about what we don't have.

This story was taken from Acts 16:11-40.

Session 6

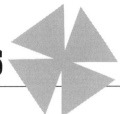

Bible Verse

Philippians 4:12

"I know what it is to be in need, and I know what it is to have plenty. I have learned the secret of being content in any and every situation, whether well fed or hungry, whether living in plenty or in want."

For younger children: "I have learned the secret of being content in any and every situation."

● ● ● ● ——————————————

Transition

Contentment is in the heart even when people are disappointed or don't get what they want. Sometimes kids ask for something and Mom or Dad says no. How do kids respond when they don't get an answer that they want? Let kids brainstorm about possible negative answers. Three common negative responses to a no answer are arguing, badgering, and whining. What might be a good response to a no answer? A child needs to learn to say "okay" instead of complaining. That's a sign of contentment. Accepting no as an answer shows maturity. We have a craft to help you remember this idea.

Craft
Dial Up for Contentment

Preparation: Prepare this craft by photocopying the two craft pages onto cardstock. Using an exacto knife, cut the doors in the top dial. Younger children will need to have the whole project cut and ready to go before they begin. You'll also need scissors, markers or crayons, brads, and something sharp to poke the hole.

Can I Accept No as an Answer?

Do I Argue? · *Do I Whine?*

Do I Badger?

Have children color the six faces. They might color all the happy faces one color and all the sad faces another color. Children can then color the top dial with an attractive border. As children cut

out the two dials be sure to remind them to watch out for the handles around the sides.

Poke a hole in the center of both dials using the sharp end of scissors or a ball point pen. Push a brad through the center and fasten to the two dials together so that they can move. Have children move the top handle so the happy side is revealed and open the doors to see the response. Then have them move the top handle so the sad side is revealed and open the doors again. Use this opportunity to talk about the difference between accepting no as an answer and doing other things like arguing, badgering, or whining.

For Younger Children

As children grow their ability to use arguing, badgering, and whining increases. Many young children won't understand arguing but most can understand whining. Badgering is a lot like begging.

● ● ● ● ——————————————

Transition

It's easy to get upset when someone tells us no. That's because in our hearts we get disappointed. Disappointment makes people sad and sometimes even angry. Everyone needs to be able to deal with disappointment. Show me a face that isn't happy. We all need to be able to accept no as an answer with a gracious heart. We need to be able to say in our hearts, "It's okay." One of the signs of maturity is that you're able to accept no as an answer. Let's practice with a game.

Activity
May I Have Your Seat Please?

Preparation: Form a circle of chairs with one less chair than the number of children.

Have children sit in the circle. One child is the "tired child in need of a chair" who stands in the center. Have the tired child go to a seated child and ask, "May I have your seat please?" The child can respond "yes" or "no." If the child responds "yes," then the seated child becomes the new tired

child in need of a chair. When the answer is "no" the child in need must give a good response and then go to someone else.

Several things can happen in this activity, giving teachers opportunities to dialogue with kids. Sometimes several children will say no, creating frustration for the tired child in need of a chair. The responses are very important. Children who think it's funny to keep saying no are being unkind and you might say, "Our tired child in need of a chair is having a hard time finding someone who is willing to be a servant and give up his chair. Who might consider giving a yes answer to our friend?" Or, if the tired child in need of a chair becomes frustrated and angry you might say, "I can see why you'd be frustrated. It looks like everywhere you turn you're getting a no answer. This is when we get to learn some things about you. Can you be content on the inside, like Paul, or do you get upset with a no answer and start getting angry?" Sometimes children are compliant, and because of the staged environment, everyone says "yes." Usually if you play the game a little longer children will begin to say no. You may want to prompt them by giving permission for the children to say no. "You can say yes or you can say no, whichever you want."

● ● ● ● ●

Transition

Some children have an automatic response to a no answer. They start arguing, or yelling, or whining. It just starts happening. That's because we've trained ourselves with bad habits. What we need is a better response. But a better response requires training as well. This next activity will help you see that you can learn a new way.

Activity
Training a Sewing Needle

Preparation: You will need a sewing needle, red fingernail polish, a styrofoam cup, a magnet, and a 6–8″ bowl filled with about 1″ of water. Photocopy and assemble the little stand up signs

at the end of this lesson that say "Arguing" "Badgering" "Whining" "Willing to Accept No as an Answer." Dip the eye end of a sewing needle into red fingernail polish to help identify it as the tail. Let it dry.

In this activity you will show children that, in the same way that a compass needle continues to move toward north, our hearts can learn to be content.

Break a small piece of styrofoam off the bottom of the cup. Place it in the water to float. Now place the sewing needle on top of the styrofoam. Take note of where the needle points to even before you magnetize it.

Take the needle off the styrofoam and use a magnet to stroke the needle by holding the red end of the needle and rubbing the magnet toward the point. Do not rub back the other way. Only rub toward the point. Do this about 20 times. You have now magnetized the needle. Place it on the styrofoam and watch it align itself in a north/south direction.

Place the little signs around the bowl with the red end of the needle pointing directly opposite the "Willing to Accept No as an Answer" Tell the children how the experiment works. The magnet sets the needle in such a way that it aligns itself with the earth's north and south. It always moves in the same direction. Children who can't accept no as an answer are just like that. They tend to move toward badgering, or whining, or arguing when they don't get what they want. Use the small stand up signs to illustrate how the pointer always floats toward arguing or badgering for example. There's good news though. You can retrain your internal compass to think differently about a no answer. Let me show you how.

Take the needle off the styrofoam and hold it by its point this time. Stroke the magnet on the needle toward the red end about 20 times and you will have reversed the polarity of magnetic force. Put the needle back on the styrofoam.

Watch the needle move slowly to the "Willing to Accept No as an Answer" direction. You have successfully retrained the needle. When children learn to accept no as an answer they can be content and say "It's okay." While the needle is moving you can ask children what kinds of things parents say no to and talk about ways that kids can accept no as an answer in those situations.

Transition

When Mom gives you a no answer, how do you respond? Do you get angry and argue? Do you just whine and try to make other people miserable? Let's practice being a parent and a child and see what happens. Remember that one of the signs of maturity is that a person can accept no as an answer.

Role Play

Preparation: Photocopy and cut apart the instructions cards at the end of this lesson.

One child plays the mom or dad and the other plays the child. The older the child, the more drama you're likely to see. Three different requests are brought to Mom and the children role-play arguing, badgering, and whining. The fourth scenario illustrates the right response. With younger children you can role play good and bad responses to a no answer by the teacher telling the stories below and then all the kids pretending to respond with badgering, whining, or arguing. Show it by body movement, facial expression, and tone of voice. Have the kids play it up and enjoy drawing attention to the negative in order to practice the positive.

Role Play 1

Child: Can I watch a movie at my friend's house? It's called "Mean Tricks to Play on Your Brother." When the parent says no, try to convince him or her anyway.

Parent: When you hear the request, say no and then try to explain to the child why it isn't a good idea. Listen to what the child says and then explain some more.

Role Play 2

Child: I know I've already had two donuts and three cookies, but my friend just gave me this candy bar. Can I eat it? When the parent says no show that you're upset by whining and complaining.

Parent: Appear shocked at your child's request and then say no. Try to comfort your child who is obviously disappointed.

Role Play 3

Child: Can I spend the night at my friend's house this Friday? When the parent says no, look for other ways to ask the question to try to get the parent to change the decision.

Parent: Tell the child no and think of a good reason why you're saying no. Try to stick to your no answer but listen to what your child has to say.

Role Play 4

Child: I know I haven't had a bath for a week but could I skip my bath again tonight so I can keep playing with my toys instead? When the parent says no then respond in a good way.

Parent: Skip your bath again? No way. You can't skip your shower. The answer is no.

Transition

I think we're getting the idea, aren't we? Some children can't accept no as an answer and then they start mistreating people. They are disappointed and they don't know how to handle it. The solution is to be more flexible and be able to accept disappointment. It's okay. It's not the end of the world. I'll make it. Maybe next time. You know, kids, people who can't accept no as an answer are often very unhappy people. One of the keys to being happy in life it to learn to accept no. It shows maturity.

Sometimes kids won't accept no as an answer and they continue to ask and ask and ask and won't stop. We call that badgering. Can someone give me an example of what badgering might look like in a

family? Allow children to explore the idea by giving examples of what some kids do to their parents in this area.

Activity
Let's Talk About Badgering

Using the picture of a badger and its paw at the end of this lesson, talk about the animal and observe some of its characteristics. It has sharp claws and teeth, a pointed nose, strong arms and paws. Then tell kids the following story about a badger:

 Usually badgers don't attack people but in Windsor, Ontario, Canada, Sergeant Stone saw a different side of this fierce little animal. He was called to a lady's home because of some noise in her garage. It turns out that a badger had given birth in some old blankets and now the mother badger was foraging around for food. The owner of the house kept a few extra food items in the garage and the badger had scattered them around the area. Melons and squash were consumed. Packages of chips and crackers were littered all over the floor. Sergeant Stone opened the door and the badger started coming toward him. He was surprised because he'd seen many badgers and they are usually afraid of people. This badger barred his teeth and so Sergeant Stone took off running toward his car. The badger followed him. A few minutes later reinforcements arrived on the scene and found the badger on the ground looking up at the policeman who was sitting on the roof of his police car. The animal control department arrived and captured the mother badger and took her and her two cubs to a safe place where they were nurtured for a time and then released again in the woods.

Use this illustration to talk about how sometimes children are compared to badgers when kids won't accept no as an answer. Sometimes children can be fierce and even mean to parents because they don't like the answer they receive to a request. Disappointment is not an excuse for meanness.

Negative responses include things like begging, crying, whining, arguing, pleading, or bartering. Positive responses require the child to say things like, "Okay, maybe next time," or "I'll try someone else," or "It's okay to not have that."

● ● ● ● ●
Transition

Children who learn to accept no as an answer demonstrate it with contentment. It's okay that we don't get everything we wish for. We sometimes need to learn how to just enjoy the things we have. In this snack children discover a recipe made of all kinds of things, but when put together they make a delicious treat. Life is like that sometimes. If you look at the challenges you face, you can often see how various pieces make an interesting concoction.

Snack
Treasure Glops

Preparation: Buy the ingredients to make the following recipe and prepare it in advance.

8 cups stick pretzels	3 cup raisins
3 cup mini-marshmallows	24 oz chocolate chips
6 cups of corn or rice Chex cereal	

Combine pretzels, raisins, cereal squares, and marshmallows into two large bowls for easier mixing. Set aside. Microwave 12 oz of chocolate chips for each bowl until melted and stir until smooth. Immediately pour melted chocolate over pretzel mixture, stirring until pieces are evenly coated. Scoop 1/2 cup servings onto wax paper covered baking sheets and refrigerate 20 minutes to harden. Makes 30 servings.

Be sure to be prepared with plenty of napkins and wipes for this snack. You might want to take pictures of children eating this rather messy snack.

This snack is made of several random ingredients. Although you wouldn't typically put these things together, they make a delightful snack. Sometimes life is like that. Various ingredients come together in rather unexpected ways. Our job is to learn how to accept them and learn to be content.

Session 6

Activity
Contentment Color Page

Preparation: Photocopy the color page at the end of this lesson. Provide markers or crayons.

Allow children to color the page while you talk about contentment and its value both in the family and elsewhere in life.

● ● ● ● ● ────────────

Review and Close

When children can't accept no as an answer they can become mean like a badger or they end up whining like a hinge on an old door. In just a moment I'm going to ask you to whine and we'll all whine together for a few seconds. When I put my hand up then I want you to stop. Okay? Ready? Whine!

After a few seconds hold up your hand to stop the whining.

Arguing, badgering, and whining are unkind responses when you don't get what you want. But they are wrong. In fact, people who can't accept no as an answer are often mean and mean people are unhappy people.

What's a better way to respond when you don't get what you want? Saying "Okay" or "Maybe next time" or just letting it go are much better. We don't have to have all the things we think we have to have. That's an important lesson for all of us to learn.

Maturity requires that a person be able to accept no as an answer, even when it's disappointing. I'd like to see you kids work on that this week and report back to me next week. We're learning about some treasures in our hearts that will help us be successful. Accepting no is one of those treasures. When we have those treasures in our hearts we can enjoy life much more.

Photocopied by permission from the National Center for Biblical Parenting

Arm Badge

I Can Accept No as an Answer!

I Can Accept No as an Answer!

I Can Accept No as an Answer!

I Can Accept No as an Answer!

I Can Accept No as an Answer!

I Can Accept No as an Answer!

Can I Accept No as an Answer?

Do I Argue?

Do I Whine?

Do I Badger?

"I know what it is to be in need, and I know what it is to have plenty. I have learned the secret of being content in any and every situation, whether well fed or hungry, whether living in plenty or in want." Philippians 4:12

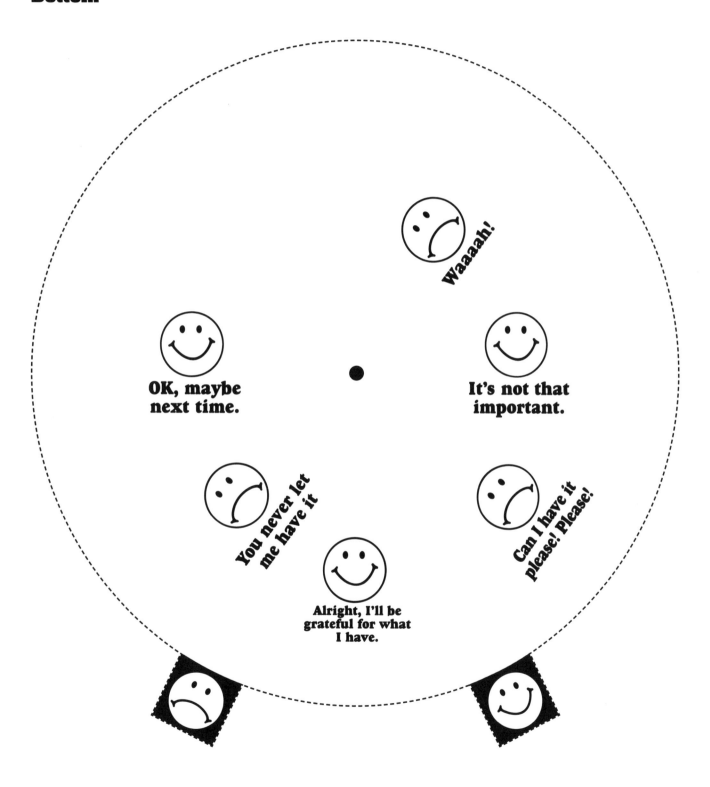

Dial Up for Contentment
Bottom

Session 6

Activity
Training a
Sewing Needle

Instructions: Cut on solid lines, fold on dotted lines to make triangular table signs. Merge the slits together at the base.

Badgering

Arguing

Badgering

Arguing

Session 6

Activity
Training a Sewing Needle

Instructions: Cut on solid lines, fold on dotted lines to make triangular table signs. Merge the slits together at the base.

Willing to Accept No as an Answer

Whining

Willing to Accept No as an Answer

Whining

Session 6

Activity
Role Play

Role Play 1

Child: Can I watch a movie at my friend's house. It's called "Mean Tricks to Play on Your Brother." When the parent says no, try to convince her or him anyway.

Role Play 1

Parent: When you hear the request, say no and then try to explain to the child why it isn't a good idea. Listen to what the child says and then explain some more.

Role Play 2

Child: I know I've already had two donuts and three cookies, but my friend just gave me this candy bar. Can I eat it? When the parent says no show that you're upset by whining and complaining.

Role Play 2

Parent: Appear shocked at your child's request and then say no. Try to comfort your child who is obviously disappointed.

Role Play 3

Child: Can I spend the night at my friend's house this Friday? When the parent says no, look for other ways to ask the question to try to get the parent to change the decision.

Role Play 3

Parent: Tell the child no and think of a good reason why you're saying no. Try to stick to your no answer but listen to what your child has to say.

Role Play 4

Child: I know I haven't had a bath for a week but could I skip my bath again tonight so I can keep playing with my toys instead? When the parent says no then respond in a good way.

Role Play 4

Parent: Skip your shower again? No way. You can't skip your shower. The answer is no.

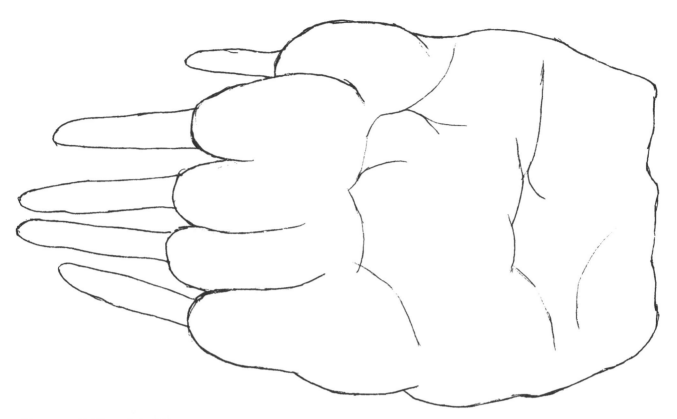

Philippians 4:12

I have learned the secret of being content.

76 Hopatcong Drive, Lawrenceville, NJ 08648-4136
(800) 771-8334 or (609) 771-8002
Email: parent@biblicalparenting.org
Web: biblicalparenting.org

Accepting No as an Answer

Dear Parent,

One of the realities of life is that parents have to set limits and say no to their kids. Unfortunately some children have difficulty accepting that answer. They then engage in all kinds of manipulative and mean techniques to get what they want. In particular, children have three negative responses: they argue, badger, and whine.

Theme: Accepting no as an answer shows maturity.

In this session we studied the story of Paul and Silas who sang in prison to illustrate the fact that even when life is hard we can respond well. Children saw a picture of a badger and we talked about how kids are often like this tenacious animal as they relate to parents. You might ask your child about how we trained a needle to move in a bowl of water. At first it pointed to arguing but as we retrained it, the needle turned from the arguing to be willing to accept no as an answer.

Our Bible verse is Philippians 4:12 "I know what it is to be in need, and I know what it is to have plenty. I have learned the secret of being content in any and every situation, whether well fed or hungry, whether living in plenty or in want."

You might reinforce the things your child learned by discussing the lesson this week. During the course of the week spend some time talking about how your child responds to disappointment and explore more mature ways to handle situations.

Blessings,

Scott Turansky   Joanne Miller
National Center for Biblical Parenting
www.biblicalparenting.org

Attitude is a Window into a Child's Heart

Preparing Your Heart to Teach Session 7

An attitude is a pre-packaged response to some kind of trigger. As you think about your own life, what kinds of triggers throw you into a bad attitude? Maybe it's when the kids get annoying, or when traffic slows you down. Maybe you have a bad attitude when someone disappoints you or when you don't get what you had hoped for. One of the challenges faced by all adults and children is identifying bad attitudes and then figuring out how to change them into good attitudes.

Attitudes are made up of three parts. Behavior is the part you see: stomping, dirty looks, tone of voice etc. It's often the behavior that reveals that a problem exists. A second part is the emotion. This is important because emotion feeds intensity. The emotion behind a bad attitude is often anger but can be something else like pride, irritation, frustration, or fear.

The third part of a bad attitude has to do with thinking errors. Sometimes we believe things that are not productive or are just plain erroneous. Sometimes we assume that kids will pick up after themselves and we get angry when they don't. Other times we wish we could go through a day without having to correct, but that's unreasonable. In order to change bad attitudes we must identify the things we believe about family life and re-evaluate them.

As you work through this lesson with your students ask yourself some important questions about your own attitudes. It will help you empathize with the children you're working with as they try to change theirs.

What Children Learn in Session 7

The goal of this lesson is to motivate children to consider their attitudes.

Theme: A good attitude takes practice.

Using games and activities children learn that attitudes contain both behavior and emotion. Behavior is what people see. The role play has children demonstrate an attitude with their actions. The emotions game has kids guessing the emotion that the child is acting out. Discussions about ways to change bad attitudes into good ones get kids thinking and the Bible story encourages children to avoid negative influences that contribute to a bad attitude. Younger children may have trouble understanding the whole concept of an attitude so specific suggestions are provided along the way.

Read Along in the Book, "Parenting is Heart Work"

Chapter 5 addresses the value of emotions. Since emotions are one part of an attitude, it's helpful to understand their purpose and how to respond well emotionally. Many children choose responses based on feelings, turning disappointment, frustration, and anger into resistance, meanness, and aggression. Instead of trying to get rid of emotions, teaching the heart means learning to sort out the good side of feelings from their negative counterparts. Chapter 12 describes ways to use the scriptures in child training. Since another part of attitudes has to do with thinking errors, continually giving children scriptural guidance allows them to develop healthy paradigms and thinking patterns.

Session 7

Theme

A good attitude takes practice.

Welcome Activity
The Mission Card

Preparation: Photocopy the Mission Card activity at the end of this lesson.
Children will each need an envelope along with markers or crayons, scissors, and glue.

Have children color the two pieces, one to be glued onto the outside of the envelope and the other to put inside. Use this opportunity to help children understand the importance of having a good attitude in life.

As you talk to children, ask them what a mission is? Make sure they understand that a mission is an assignment to do something or it's a special job that you have. A good attitude is important in a family and essential for anyone who wants to be successful in life.

Today we're going to talk about attitudes. We all have them. Some are good and some are bad. Sometimes I have a bad attitude and I need to understand how to turn it into a good attitude. In this lesson we're going to show you how you can do the same thing.

● ● ● ● ● ──────────

Together Time

Use the ideas below along with your own thoughts and the Bible to dialogue with the children and help them see that they can change their attitudes and that an attitude can either have a positive or negative impact on their lives.

Object Lesson
The Attractive Dirty Mug

Preparation: Find a nice looking, attractive mug or non-transparent cup. Put mud all over the inside. Have a dishpan ready with soap and water to clean the mug later in the story.

I would like to show you my favorite mug. Isn't this a nice mug? I like it because it has pretty colors or the words say something special, or it's shaped nicely. Do any of you have a favorite cup or mug you like to use? Who would like to drink out of my mug? It sure looks good on the outside doesn't it? Take a look on the inside. Who would like to drink out of my mug now? That's gross isn't it? I'm going to put my mug aside here for a minute.

Bible Story
Bad Influences for Jesus' Disciples

Jesus loved his disciples. He wanted them to be successful in life. He looked for ways to teach them the right way to live. Who can tell us a sport you like to play? Allow a few children to share their sports activities. The coach of a soccer team or a basketball team has a goal—to help the team win. The coach knows more ways to win and has ideas and strategies to help the players be successful. Jesus was like a coach to his disciples, coaching them along so that they could grow in their faith.

Parents are coaches for their kids. They want their kids to win in life and they tell their kids how to be successful. Parents know more about life and they know what works and what doesn't. Sometimes a parent sees a child being lazy and the parent knows that if that child continues to be lazy, he won't be successful, so the parent coaches the child along to learn how to work hard.

Jesus saw a problem that might effect his disciples. There were some men who were always hanging around. They were called Pharisees. They looked like they were doing the right thing, but on the inside they did the wrong thing. Why do you think Jesus was concerned about having those men hang around his disciples? Yes, because they might have a bad influence on his disciples. Jesus knew that his disciples were in danger and he wanted to warn them. As is always true in life, there are some people you better be careful of.

Let me tell you a little more about the Pharisees. The Pharisees always wanted people to look at them. They weren't very humble. When they gave their money in the offering, they wanted everyone to see how much they were giving. They would look around to make sure everyone was watching and then they would pour their bag of coins into the offering to impress other people. That's wrong because God wants us to give to him, not just make a show.

Here's another thing the Pharisees liked to do. They would stand up in the synagogue and they would pray to God, "God, I'm glad I'm not like that man over there who's a tax collector." So the Pharisees would look down on people who weren't as good as them. Pharisees were proud and they put other people down. Sometimes they would make people feel bad by their comments.

Jesus was concerned. He knew that if his disciples started doing some of those things they wouldn't

be successful in life. So Jesus warned his disciples. He said, "Be careful of the Pharisees. They are hypocrites." Do you know what a hypocrite is? It's someone who pretends to be something on the outside but is really something different on the inside.

The influence of the Pharisees was dangerous because the disciples might start doing some of the same things that the Pharisees did. That would not be good.

Boys and girls, sometimes other kids don't do the right thing, do they? If you hang around with a child who does the wrong thing then maybe you'll start doing the wrong thing too. That wouldn't be good. Jesus was very concerned about his disciples. He wanted to warn them so he thought of a way he could teach his disciples about the bad things that the Pharisees were doing.

Pick up the dirty cup that looks good on the outside but is dirty on the inside. Jesus told the disciples. "Be careful of those Pharisees. They're like a cup that is clean on the outside but dirty on the inside." Show kids the inside of your cup. It might look good to be with them but don't be fooled.

Begin washing the cup in the dishpan while you continue. Kids, when you find that you've developed a bad attitude, it's important to clean it out. Just like drinking out of a dirty cup would be terrible, having a bad attitude pollutes relationships. It's important to get your attitude cleaned up so that you can be more effective in life.

Joey saw some kids having a good time. He went over to them to see what they were doing. They were laughing and making fun of one of the teachers at school. Should Joey hang around these guys or should he get out of there? You're right. He should get out of there quickly, because if he doesn't he might start becoming like those kids who are doing the wrong thing.

Be careful who you hang around with. Today we're going to talk about a bad attitude. Some kids have a bad attitude and when you hang around them you start to develop a bad attitude

too. Just like Jesus warned his disciples about the Pharisees, we need to be warned about staying away from kids who have bad attitudes or who are doing the wrong thing.

For Younger Children

Younger children will likely have a difficult time understanding what an attitude is, but talking about being grumpy or mean is certainly something they can catch. Younger kids also like the dirty cup illustration and can understand the importance of changing their pouting into happy faces or anger into cooperation.

This Bible story was taken from Matthew 23:1-28.

Bible Verse

Proverbs 15:30
"A cheerful look brings joy to the heart, and good news gives health to the bones."

● ● ● ● ● ——————————

Transition

One of the challenges with attitudes is that they sneak up on you. They seem to be automatic at times. Before you even realize it you're stuck with that same response over and over again. It takes work to change bad attitudes. But first we have to see what starts them off. In this next activity we're going to have some fun looking at the cues that bring on bad attitudes.

Activity (For Older Children)
Saturday Morning Attitudes

Divide the children into four groups. Explain that sometimes we have pre-packaged responses to triggers and cues in life. For example, if your brother pokes you, you might hit him back. You don't even think about it. You just do it even if it isn't the right thing to do. It takes work to change some of those automatic responses. That, in part, is what maturity is all about.

We're going to play a game. In a moment I'm going to read a story about a Saturday morning. As I read the story I want you to listen for your cue and then you'll respond.

Group 1 Listen for the word "work" or "clean" and when you hear it, I want you to groan with a sigh "Uhhh."

Group 2 Listen for "I want you to" and when you hear it, you roll your eyes and chin and say "Sst Huh" (tongue clicks with teeth and then exhale in disgust)

Group 3 Listen for the word "No" and you say "But Dad" in a whiny voice.

Group 4 Listen for the word "now" and you say, "not yet!"

Practice with each group to make sure they're ready. Then have fun by reading the story at the end of this lesson. Play it up with the kids so they exaggerate their responses.

After the story talk to the kids about the automatic responses they have in family life. Sometimes Mom asks you to help out and you groan or complain. That's a bad attitude. It takes work to change.

● ● ● ● ● ——————————

Transition

One of the ways to change bad attitudes into good ones is to set up some new cues. These reminders get you moving in the right direction so that you can form a good attitude. For some it's listening to praise music, laughing, praying, or remembering a favorite Bible verse. In our craft today we want to make a reminder to help you remember to have a good attitude.

Craft
Stained Glass Window

Preparation: In advance use an exacto knife or pair of scissors to shave a few different color crayons. Also cut up small pieces of aluminum foil and colored tissue paper. Photocopy the attitude page at the end of this lesson. You'll also need two 9"x 12"(approximately) pieces of wax paper per

ATTITUDE

child, an iron and ironing board, cardstock or construction paper, a towel, a cookie sheet, some yarn, and a hole punch.

Note: This craft is special for the kids but requires quite a bit of adult involvement. You may want to have a few extra helpers to make sure things run smoothly.

Introduce this craft by telling the children that an attitude is a window into a person's heart. We're going to create a stained glass window to use as a reminder to have a good attitude.

Have children cut out the word "Attitude" from the template at the end of this lesson. Older children can cut all around the black letters. Younger kids can just cut around the whole word. Kids can then place that word on one piece of wax paper (wax side up) and sprinkle the other ingredients around it. Place a second piece of wax paper (wax side down) over the top. One at a time an assistant can slide one child's craft onto a cookie sheet and bring it to the teacher to iron. Slide the craft onto the ironing board. Place a paper towel or piece of newspaper over the wax paper and iron the craft. The heat will melt the crayon and the wax in the wax paper and it all sticks together.

Children can then put a frame around the craft made out of cardstock or construction paper. It might be best to have these frames precut with a one inch border around the outside. Children can decorate the border. Punch two holes and run yarn through the holes for hanging near a window so light can shine through.

Talk to kids about their attitudes and how a nice attitude brings joy into a room like a nice decoration does. Have several children hold their craft and smile for a picture.

● ● ● ● ● ——————————————

Transition

Where are you going to hang your attitude reminder? Allow children to brainstorm about the places they might put it. To further explore this idea of attitude we want to see that a person's posture and tone of voice often reveal what's going on in the heart.

Role Play

One of the components of an attitude has to do with behavior. Certain actions tell others that a bad attitude is inside the heart. Boys and girls, how can you tell when someone is having a bad attitude? What kinds of things do you see? After hearing a few answers, tell children, "I want you to show me a bad attitude. Everyone stand up and in just a moment altogether we're going to show a bad attitude. But first we're going to show a good attitude."

I want you to say these words, "It's a great day" and when you do, I want you to show me a good attitude. That means that the way you stand, what you do with your hands, your face, and your voice will all show me that you are having a good attitude. Let's do it together. "It's a great day."

Now I want you to show me a bad attitude. We're going to say the same words but we'll say them with sarcasm and an unhappy voice. Think about how you're going to show me a bad attitude with the way you stand, what you do with your arms, your face, and your voice. Here we go. "It's a great day."

Have everyone sit down and ask an adult or teen assistant to come up and act out a bad attitude. Ask the children, "What do you see that tells you that we have a bad attitude?" Identify the specific cues like a bottom lip stuck out or arms folded or angry eyes. The more cues you can identify the better because children will then recognize these cues in themselves.

Now we're learning the difference between a good and a bad attitude. I need a volunteer to come up and demonstrate a bad and then a good attitude. I'm going to tell you to sit down and you show me an attitude. Go ahead and obey me but do it in a way that demonstrates a bad attitude. Now do the same thing with a good attitude Now let's walk around the room with a bad attitude. Do the same with a good attitude.

People can see your attitude by the way you act. A good attitude takes practice.

Session 7

Transition

One of the things that makes attitudes a challenge is that they have emotions attached to them. What we feel influences how we think and act. When we understand our emotions better, we can manage them carefully and move into positive attitudes more easily.

Game (For Older Children)
Guess the Emotion

Preparation: Photocopy onto cardstock the four "Guess the Emotion" pages at the end of this lesson. Cut them into cards. Copy the emotion cards onto a different color from the statement cards.

Put the cards in two piles. Ask for a volunteer to come up, take one card from each pile and then say the words on the statement card while expressing the emotion on the other. The class must try to guess the emotion. Coach the volunteer with ways to express the emotion.

Isn't it interesting that we communicate what we're feeling through our voice and our actions? That's why attitude is so important. If you're feeling frustrated that your mom won't allow you to watch the video and then you show her that frustration it may come out in some pretty mean ways. It's important to learn how to control emotions so that you don't mistreat other people with a bad attitude.

Game (For Younger Children)
Guess the Emotion

Preparation: Photocopy the emotion sheet at the end of this lesson, and create one set of cards for each child to take home.

Talk about all the emotions and then have a child pick one card and try to act it out while others guess.

Attitudes have feelings so it's important for children to develop more healthy ways to communicate their feelings rather than just showing a bad attitude. Use this activity to talk about feeling and give children ideas about ways that emotions can be communicated without being mean or hurtful.

Transition

Some children have a real problem with bad attitudes. Almost anything you say to them results in some kind of mean comment. I want to show you a fun science activity that demonstrates what a bad attitude looks like with some kids.

Activity
Film Canister with an Attitude

Preparation: In advance obtain several film canisters. Be sure to get the kind where the lid fits inside the canister like Fuji film because they work the best. You can usually get these from the local film processing center. Also obtain Alka Seltzer tablets and break them into 1/4 pieces. Create a launcher by cutting three slits about one inch long in the end of a toilet paper tube. Bend the slits out so that you can tape them to a paper plate. Fasten the cartoon boy from the end of this lesson onto the toilet paper roll.

Fill the canisters 1/3 full with water and set them down on the table. Talk about attitude with children by saying something like the following. "Some kids have a bad attitude. When a mom says no you can't go to your friend's house or no you can't eat candy right now, they start being miserable and taking it out on people. They start moping around the house or treating other people unkindly. Let's imagine that this plastic canister is the heart and that this tablet here is the bad attitude and that this toilet paper tube is Johnny.

Let's say that Mom asks him to do something and he doesn't want to. Let's see what happens. Johnny, no you can't go over to Jack's house today."

Drop the 1/4 tablet of Alka Seltzer into one film canister. Snap the lid tightly into the canister and drop it into the toilet paper launcher, lid down, and stand back. Continue to ask Johnny to go out and rake the leaves, or clean up his room. It usually takes 20-30 seconds before the canister shoots into the air. The kids will be amazed at the explosion.

Continue with the second canister. "Johnny, that's not a good response. I want you to clean up your room. We're having company over later." Drop the next canister of water and Alka Seltzer into the tube while you continue to ask Johnny to do the right thing.

"Johnny. I don't like your attitude. I want you to take a Break and settle down." After the second explosion drop the third canister in while you talk about the importance of having a good response to correction. Of course Johnny doesn't because he explodes again.

As you'll discover, it's best to do this activity outdoors or with a high ceiling, although bouncing canisters off the ceiling also has an effect.

Does this demonstration remind you of how you respond with a bad attitude sometimes? I hope you'll consider controlling your emotions and changing your bad attitudes into good ones as you live in your family this week.

● ● ● ● ● ───────

Transition

Ask kids, "When you're stuck in a bad attitude, how do you get out of it?" Allow children to share their ideas. People have different ways of handling bad attitudes and turning them into good attitudes. We're going to have a snack now and this snack is great. In fact, it's called, Brownies with Attitude.

Snack
Brownies with Attitude

Preparation: Buy brownies or make the delicious ones from this recipe.

Brownie Recipe

1 cup butter or margarine
4 ounces unsweetened chocolate
4 eggs
2 cups sugar
2 teaspoons vanilla
1 1/2 cups all-purpose flour
2 cups mini-marshmallows
1 cup chocolate chips

Melt butter and chocolate over a low heat. Place in bowl with eggs, sugar and vanilla. Mix lightly until combined and then mix in flour. Spread the batter in greased 9x13x2 baking pan. Bake at 350° for 30-35 minutes. Take out of the oven and sprinkle mini-marshmallows and chocolate chips on top. Bake for about 2-3 more minutes. Cool and cut. Makes approximately 36 brownies. Serve with a smile.

It doesn't take much sometimes to change a bad attitude into a good attitude. These brownies are a good example. If you came into the room with a bad attitude, then sit down, take a deep breath, close your eyes, imagine a warm beach somewhere, quote a Bible verse, list three things you're grateful for, and then eat a brownie, everything changes. You walk out of the room floating on air ready to show love to everyone around. If that for some reason doesn't work, then do it all again. These brownies are amazing.

Session 7

Review and Close

I hope you're getting some ideas for working on your attitudes. Bad attitudes tend to happen in three areas. First they happen when children are given an instruction that they'd rather not do such as clean up their room or take out the trash. A second time we see bad attitudes is when children are corrected. Stop fighting with your brother. You need to apologize for the way you talked. The third way that kids demonstrate a bad attitude is when they don't get what they want. The answer is no. Whew! Then we can see a bad attitude too.

Think for a moment when it is that you struggle the most with a bad attitude. It's important to stop and think about what the trigger is. You'll also want to see if you can figure out what emotion is behind it all. Then you'll want to change the way you think and act so that you don't have a bad attitude. In fact, a real sign of maturity is someone who can have a good attitude when challenges come around and when things aren't going well. Those people have really made some progress with their attitudes. Remember: A good attitude takes practice.

Session 7

Outside

Inside

BURN YOUR MIND YOUR BRIDGES

Practice Having a GOOD ATTITUDE

"A cheerful look brings joy to the heart, and good news gives health to the bones."
Proverbs 15:30

Treasure Hunter

Session 7

Saturday Morning Attitudes

It's Saturday. Everyone knew that this would be a Saturday to **work** (**Uhhhh**) in the yard. Dad had some extra time so he started to trim the bushes. He had been outside for about an hour and decided it was time to have his two children, Carl age 10, and Karen, age 12, join him.

"Carl, come on outside please."

"Yes," Carl said looking out the window.

"I want you to help me in the yard." (**Sst Huh**)

Carl was having a difficult time getting himself going this morning. He liked to get involved in projects and often had a hard time switching to something when asked.

"Carl, we've got a lot of things to **clean** up." (**Uhhh**). "**I want you** to come outside." (**Sst Huh**). "We can get a lot of **work** done today." (**Uhhh**).

Carl turned away from the window and then turned back and said, "Could I play on the computer a little longer?"

His dad looked up at him and said, **"No."** (**But Dad**). "We're going to do this **work,** (**Uhhh**) **now.** (**Not yet**).

Once Carl came out, Dad said, **"I want you to** get a broom..." (**Sst Huh**) "and **clean** the sidewalk." (**Uhhh**)

"Where's the broom?" Carl asked.

"Check in the shed and see if you can find it."

"Couldn't you get it for me, Dad? I'm tying my shoe."

"No, ("But Dad") "I want you to go find it." (**Sst Huh**).

Just then Karen came home from her friend's house. "What are you guys doing?" she asked. Today is the day we're going to get some things done around here. We could use your help. **I want you to** rake those leaves." (**Sst Huh**)

"Could I sweep instead, Dad?"

"No." (**But Dad**).

"Look you guys. After we get all done we're going to play and have some fun together, but **now** (**Not yet**) I want you to (**Sst Huh**) **work.**" (**Uhhh**) "Let's not have any more complaining. We're going to **work** (**Uhhh**) for awhile. **I want you to** (**Sst Huh**) do it **now.**" (**Not yet**)

After you work through the story using these negative cues you might want to go back and add positive cues to play up a good attitude. This is especially fun for older children because some of the answers seem so unusual from kids today. Group 1: Sure!, Group 2: Yes Dad. Group 3: Okay, Group 4: all right.

You can also do this activity with flash cards and have the whole group look for cues. The flash cards would contain both the positive and negative responses as you work through the story.

Photocopied by permission from the National Center for Biblical Parenting

ATTITUDE

ATTITUDE

ATTITUDE

ATTITUDE

Game (For Older Children)
Guess the Emotion - Emotion Cards

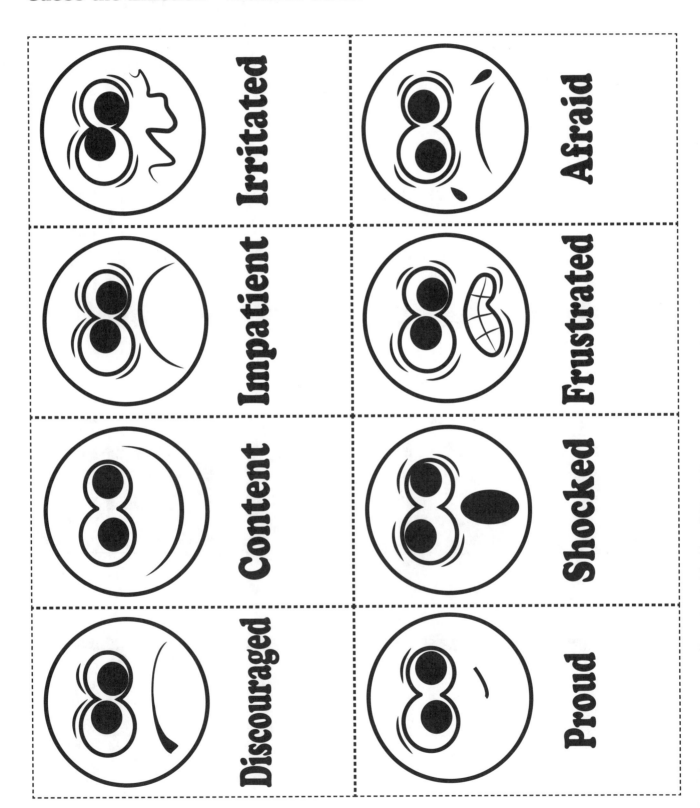

Game (For Older Children)
Guess the Emotion - Emotion Cards

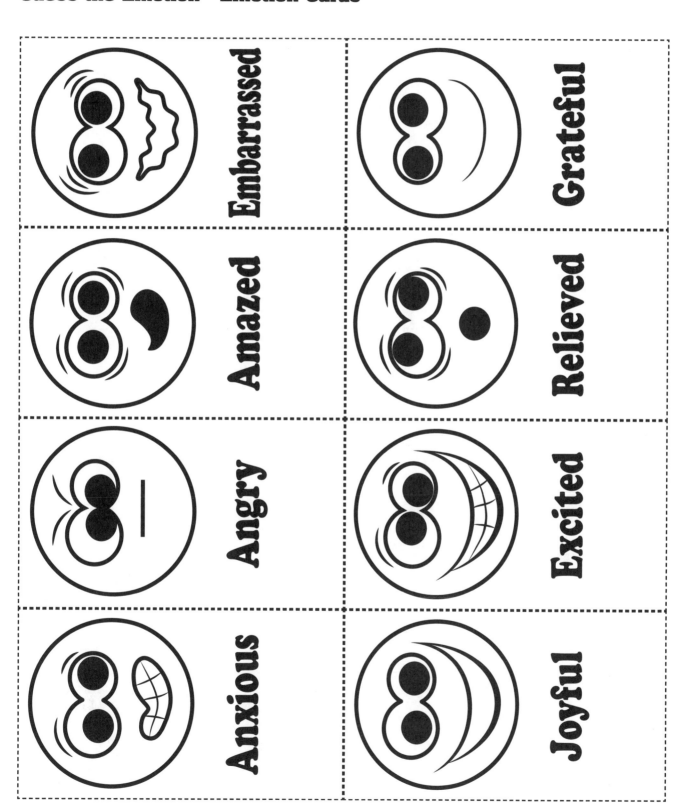

Embarrassed

Grateful

Amazed

Relieved

Angry

Excited

Anxious

Joyful

Game (For Older Children)
Guess the Emotion - Statement Cards

My mom cooked lasagna for dinner.	Our power went out and so I read a book by candlelight.
When I get older I'm going to go to college.	We got a new game at home and it has a lot of ways to play it.
We were in the restaurant when the police came in.	My brother and I played a game and he won.
The trash truck broke down right in front of our house.	In my bedroom I have three pieces of furniture.

Game (For Older Children)
Guess the Emotion - Statement Cards

I love chocolate ice cream.	**Today we had a fire truck come to our school.**
I scored three goals at the soccer game.	**The mailman didn't bring that letter I was expecting.**
My dad told me that we're taking a vacation in the mountains this year.	**I spent my weekend digging for buried treasure.**
The shoes I'm wearing I got from my cousin.	**The tree in front of our house fell over last night.**

Game (For Younger Children)
Guess the Emotion

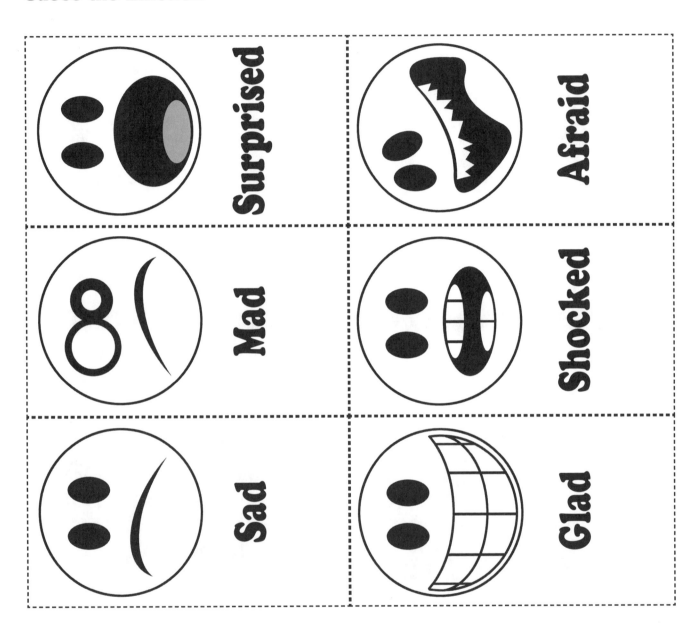

Film Canister Rocket Activity

76 Hopatcong Drive, Lawrenceville, NJ 08648-4136
(800) 771-8334 or (609) 771-8002
Email: parent@biblicalparenting.org
Web: biblicalparenting.org

Dealing With Attitudes

Dear Parent,

Have you ever struggled with a bad attitude in your child? Most parents have. It's amazing how kids can develop what seems to be an automatic response to correction, requests, or a no answer. Bad attitudes are a problem. They hinder closeness in relationships and regularly slow down progress in the tasks necessary of family life.

Theme: A good attitude takes practice.

We demonstrated what a bad attitude is using an exploding film canister and we talked about ways that emotions feed bad attitudes. As we looked at the Bible we focused on Jesus' warning to his disciples to avoid the prideful attitude of the Pharisees. In doing so, we talked to children about the influences in their own lives that might contribute to a bad attitude. The verse for this lesson is Proverbs 15:30 to illustrate the importance of our attitudes and their effect on others.

In this session we played several games to help children understand that their behavior indicates an attitude, that emotions feed attitudes, and that attitudes can be changed. In one of the games we had children act out an emotion and we all tried to guess what it was. Helping children understand and communicate emotions in healthy ways is one of the solutions for bad attitude problems in family life.

The Attitude Window Craft is a fun way to help children remember that they can change their attitudes. Sometimes it means they just have to look out the window and get a different perspective. And of course, you'll want to ask your child about the Brownies with Attitude we enjoyed.

Attitudes aren't easy to change in children or parents. They are pre-packaged responses to common triggers. Continued work in this area though produces helpful results. Be sure to pray for your child often. Remember, God is interested in the heart of your child and he is working on changing it. You are just one of the tools he'll use.

Blessings,

Scott Turansky   Joanne Miller
National Center for Biblical Parenting
www.biblicalparenting.org

Learning to Value My Family

Preparing Your Heart to Teach Session 8

Relationships require work. It's an investment. You have to listen when you'd rather read, communicate when you'd rather go on to something else, and take time to think about what the other person is feeling and experiencing. The result is a friendship that grows and develops.

Relationships with children require the same kind of investment. With all the busyness of life, relational time can get pushed to the background. Although this may be expedient in the short run, over time it takes its toll. Every person must look for ways to add emotional energy to family life.

Take a moment and consider relationships that you're investing in right now. What are you doing to contribute to their strength? Typically that means extra time and thoughtfulness. An extra phone call, a word of encouragement, a tender moment, or a listening ear may be just what it takes to touch someone else's heart.

As you go through this lesson consider your own relationships. You may think about relationships with children, your spouse, neighbors, or co-workers. On any level the thoughts in this lesson will enhance the relationships you have with others.

What Children Learn in Session 8

Many children lack the initiative to add to family life. Kids can be quite self-centered at times and only do what is required or resist any attempts at cooperation. In this lesson children receive a vision for doing more to strengthen their own family. Focus is placed on listening and thinking about others' interests and not just their own.

Theme: My family is a treasure.

During the lesson children learn to listen like Mary did instead of making Martha's mistake of focusing on her own agenda. The Bible verse encourages children to consider others. Games, activities, and a snack help children see that they can do a lot to enhance the emotional climate of family life.

Read along in the book, "Parenting is Heart Work"

A heart-based approach to working with children begins by looking for ways to open up a child's heart. Soft hearts are teachable hearts. Chapter 6 offers several practical ideas for softening a child's heart through emotional connectedness. Chapter 8 teaches some important communication skills and discusses how to use the Gratefulness Principle in family life. Children need to develop gratefulness in their lives. It's a heart quality and a higher form of motivation than the reward/punishment model children often seem to require.

Session 8

Theme

My family is a treasure.

Welcome Activity
Greeting Cards

Preparation: Photocopy the greeting cards at the end of this lesson and cut them out, one or two cards per child.

Have children decorate the card and talk about who they are going to give it to and how. Use the treasure theme to talk about how valuable a family is and that showing people that you care is a way to encourage them. Kids will likely need help knowing how to start the card with "Dear _____," and then "Thank you for…" or "I like the way you…" or just "I love you." Younger children will require help writing the text inside the card.

Together Time

Use the ideas below along with your own thoughts and the Bible to dialogue with the children and help them see that relationships are important and that listening to others is a way to express value.

Object Lesson
A Listening Exercise

Preparation: Bring a paper bag of objects that make a recognizable sound. You might choose things like opening a can of soda, spraying a spray bottle, scissors opening and shutting, a ball point pen clicking in and out, and keys jingling.

Have children be quiet and listen carefully. Use one object at a time to make a noise and have the children try to guess what it is. Talk about how listening is one of the ways we learn. Some people are too busy to listen or they like to do a lot of talking and they don't listen. Today's story from the Bible talks about the importance of listening.

Bible Story
The Better Thing

Mary, Martha, and Lazarus were brother and sisters and they all lived in the same home in Bethany, about two miles away from Jerusalem. Jesus would often visit in their home to rest and he enjoyed spending time with them.

One day they decided to host a dinner and Jesus was the honored guest. While the dinner was prepared and served people talked including Lazarus who was sitting and enjoying the guests. Martha was serving the meal.

At that moment a very interesting thing happened. Mary came in and brought with her a small container of very expensive perfume. She knelt down by Jesus, broke open the container, and poured the expensive perfume on his feet. Then she wiped his feet with her long hair. How would you feel if someone did that to you? Do you know why she did that? She was so grateful for Jesus. She loved him a lot. He had done so much for her and she wanted to show how much she loved him. One of the things that Jesus did for her was he raised her brother Lazarus from the dead. It was a very special moment for Mary.

Judas, one of the disciples, was watching all this and he shook his head in disgust. "I can't believe it," he said. "If she wanted to do something useful with that perfume, she could have taken it out and sold it. Then the money could have been given to the poor."

Judas wasn't really interested in helping the poor but he didn't see the value in what Mary was doing. In fact, Judas himself would betray Christ to be crucified. Judas was more concerned about the money than he was in the relationship between Mary and Jesus. That's a mistake. Whenever money becomes more important than relationship, you have a problem.

Jesus said to Judas, "Leave her alone." Jesus defended Mary who valued the relationship she had with Jesus.

Another time Jesus was in the same home. He and the disciples were passing through and so Jesus stopped at their home again. While there, Martha

Session 8

began preparing a meal. In fact, she had a lot to do to get things ready. She had to set the table, decide what she was going to make for dinner, cook it all and serve it. As she was working hard she saw that her sister, Mary, wasn't helping at all. In fact, Mary was sitting by Jesus and just listening and listening.

Martha started to get aggravated and annoyed at Mary. She started thinking, "This isn't fair. I have to do all the work and Mary just sits over there and listens to Jesus." After a little while Martha went in to the room, looked right at Jesus, and said, "Don't you care that I have to do all the work. Tell my sister to come and help me get the food ready."

Now, Jesus had to make a choice. First of all, getting the food ready was important. But was that the most important thing? Mary was also doing something important. She was enjoying being with Jesus and she was showing that by listening. So Jesus decided that this was a time to teach Martha a very important lesson.

Jesus turned to Martha and said, "You are worried and upset about many things. Mary has chosen something better." What is the better thing that Mary chose? It was listening to Jesus. Listening is so important because it means that you value the relationship with that person.

Boys and girls, the relationship you have with your mom and dad is very important. Sometimes we're like Martha focused on doing whatever we want to do, playing with our game, reading our book, or watching TV. What do you do to build relationship with your mom or dad?

One fun thing is to ask parents a question and then listen to their answers. You might ask, "What's your favorite food?" or "What do you like about your job?" Of course, the easy thing is to ask the question. The hard thing is to listen to the answer. It takes a person with a lot of love to listen to someone else talk. Most people like to talk and think about themselves. The person who can listen is a real treasure. Listening is a way to show someone that you love them because you think more about their interests than your own.

This Bible story was taken from John 12:1-8 and Luke 10:38-42.

Bible Verse
Philippians 2:4
"Each of you should look not only to your own interests, but also to the interests of others."

● ● ● ● ● ——————

Transition
Over the past several weeks children have learned a lot. This lesson has some review elements in it including the following craft. Ask children what they remember about your times together. Maybe they'll remember some of th science experiments or tell you where they've put some of the crafts. Show kids an example of the finished craft and go over the themes on the sign posts to remind children of the lessons.

Craft
Footprints to the Treasure

Preparation: Provide finger paint or tempera paint in small trays or paper plates. Enlarge the sheet at the end of this lesson to fit on an 11x17 piece of paper. Have a tub of warm water, soap, and a towel for clean up.

Session 8

Explain to children that this craft represents a review of all that they've learned. They'll be able to take this home to remind them of the success principles you've talked about. But before they take it home, they need to create mini-footprints on the paper. Have the child make a fist and place that fist, pinky side down into the paint and then make an impression on the paper. Then take one finger and make the toes. Repeat this using the other hand with a total of four or five footprints on the path to the treasure. Talk about the different kinds of treasures we learn in family life.

Transition

Sometimes kids can't see their moms and dads as a treasure. That's sad. In fact, some kids view their parents as roadblocks preventing them from having fun. It's important to see the treasure in family life. This next activity illustrates that sometimes it's hard to see something valuable.

Activity
Secret Handwriting with Invisible Ink

Preparation: Squeeze a lemon wedge into a cup or bowl. Take a small watercolor paint brush and, using the lemon juice, paint a message on a plain sheet of paper. You could write the lesson theme or just write the word "treasure." Then wash the paint brush and use it to paint other water marks on the paper to disguise the lemon juice handwriting. Be careful with the water not to touch any place where there's lemon juice. Allow the paper to dry completely. You will also need a candle and matches.

Tell children that over the past eight weeks we've been on a treasure hunt. We've made funny glasses and binoculars to take with us, a treasure map, and even a treasure chest. Today I want to show you some secret writing.

Here's what I've done. On this piece of paper I've written a secret message. I used invisible ink so that you can't read it right now. It just looks like a piece of paper that got wet. The words on this piece of paper are very important. They tell me something about a treasure. But I can't see them because they are invisible. The way to make them visible is to put them near a flame. So stand back and watch the letters appear on the paper.

Holding the paper with two hands move the back of the paper close to the candle's flame, not enough to burn the paper, but close enough to burn the lemon juice. The letters appear as a brown color on the paper.

Then take time to tell the children how it works. This invisible ink was made with lemon juice. I squeezed the lemon into a bowl and used a paint brush to put my invisible ink on this paper. The flame is hot and it doesn't take much heat to turn lemon juice brown.

The important point I want you to understand here, boys and girls, is that many times we're like Martha and we're busy doing our own thing. We don't realize what's most important. It's like we look at a piece of paper and it's just plain. If we knew the truth though we'd understand the real message that many people miss. Your family is a treasure and relationships are important.

Transition

What do you do to add to family life? One of the things you can do is invite your family to play a game. In this next activity we're going to create a game that you can take home and have people in your family play. As you invite them to play you'll be bringing joy into your family.

Activity
Shooting Frog Game

Preparation:
Obtain two different size straws. One with a larger diameter hole than the other. Each child will need several

of the smaller straws and 1/2 of the larger straw. Photocopy onto cardstock the frog page at the end of this lesson. Sealable plastic bags are helpful for taking the game home. Provide small and large paper clips, crayons, scotch tape, and scissors.

Have children take the 1/2 large straw and bend 1/2 inch of one end over and tape it to itself to seal it off. Each child should cut out one frog and color it. Tape the straw on the back of the frog right along the center median. Place a paper clip or two on the front end, between the eyes of the frog for ballast in order to get the frog to actually fly. Be sure to make a model in advance so that you can see how to evenly tape the straw for balance and give the frog some downward pitch with the paper clips on the end. The weight of the paper is an important factor as well. (You may want to distribute the "shooting straws" at the end to remove the temptation to shoot the frog before you're ready.)

Also cut out the instruction card and put it into the plastic bag along with one straw for each member of the family. To give children a little idea of the fun of this game you can have kids all line up and shoot their frogs and see whose can go the farthest. Don't play the game so much that it gets ruined though. The fun is taking it home and playing the game with other family members.

Take a moment and read the card that gives instructions of how to play the game. Tell the children that if they are considering the interests of others then the whole point of the game is to watch other people have fun and not have to be the center of attention. This is a game that's fun to watch too, not just fun to play.

● ● ● ● ● ─────────

Transition

The family works best when everyone is working together as a team. Sometimes kids resist parents and don't work as a team and then the whole family suffers. We have to learn how to work as a team. That's why we're going to play this fun team building activity.

Activity
Crossing the
Dangerous Minefield

Preparation: Obtain two pillows. You may want more pillows if you want to do this activity with more teams at one time.

Kids, I need a team of three brave souls. We have a difficult task in front of us today and it requires that we get three people safely from one side of the room to the other. Unfortunately this room is filled with explosives that will go off if you step on them. So we have these special pillows that will help us get from one side to the other. All three kids have to get on one pillow on one side of the room. Then they have to put the other pillow down and everyone must step on that pillow without touching the floor. Then they must pick up the first pillow and put it down for all three people to take the next step and so on until they can touch the wall on the other side. If a child fails and steps off the pillow that child will be blown up and the next team will get to try.

After this high energy game have the kids sit down right where they are and ask, "Why did I have you play this fun game? What is the lesson I'm trying to communicate?" The answer of course is that teamwork is essential if we want to win. The same thing is true in family life.

● ● ● ● ● ─────────

Transition

One of the ways that we demonstrate teamwork is by listening to others. Here's another game we're going to play that requires that we all listen to each other. Let's see who the good listeners are in this group.

Game
Find Your
Animal Partner

Preparation: Photocopy the animal cards at the end of this lesson. Be sure

to make two copies of each page. Cut out the cards and only use enough cards as you have children. Make sure that in the end you only use pairs of cards to make sure that everyone has a match.

Shuffle the cards and distribute them, one to each child. Tell children that they are to hide their card after they look at it so that no one knows what animal they are. Then all children are to spread out around the room and start making a noise like that animal to see if they can find their match. Tell children that when they find their match they should stop right there and sit down and watch others try to get matched up. This is another high-energy game that is a lot of fun. After you get all done, you may want to gather the cards, mix them up, redistribute them and try again.

The important lesson in this game is that you have to listen and talk in order for communication to take place. Kids often don't listen well. They just think about what they want to talk about. You are helping them learn to listen more effectively. That will help them be more successful in life and especially in their families. Grab your camera and take a picture to add to your photo diary.

Transition

Every family has special traditions that they enjoy together. Some families like to eat out for Chinese food or stop at McDonald's. Others enjoy taking a vacation or celebrating birthdays in a special way. Each family has their own special traditions. Let me read you the story of the Carlsons. They have three kids and a mom and a dad and Billy now is twelve years old. He tells the story.

One of the things we've really enjoyed as a family is telling stories. My dad is a great story teller but we all like to tell stories too. Just the other day we had a special family night. My mom made this caramel and chocolate dip and we were able to dip small marshmallows and fruit into it. We all sat around and ate the fun treat and we laughed and laughed as different people told stories. It was a great time.

Snack
Carmel and Chocolate Dip

Preparation: Cut up pieces of apple and banana into one-inch pieces. Also provide some mini-marshmallows. Purchase Chocolate and Caramel Sundae Topping, the kind that would be good for dipping fruit. Provide toothpicks for serving.

Pour puddles of sundae topping onto plates for the kids. Allow children to dip fruit and marshmallows and eat them as a snack. You might ask the question, "What are some fun things that you and your family do together?" Listen to the responses and enjoy the stories as you eat the special snack.

Review and Close

Every family is unique. In some families, children live with two parents and in other families they live with one. Sometimes grandparents help raise children and other times children are adopted into a new family. Each family has special ways of doing things, specific rules that make that family work and of course, every person in that family is valuable.

God placed you in your family so that you can learn and grow. A family is a treasure. In fact, in a family correction takes place, instructions happen, and kids learn to accept no as an answer. In short, a family is a place where all of us learn to be successful in life. You are learning that too. Of course, some kids take longer to learn these important lessons of family life.

You might want to go back and review some of the important things you've learned in these lessons. All of the themes are on the craft with the footprints. If you work on those eight things you'll be a treasure in life. That's what God wants for you and he's placed you in a family to practice and grow.

Of course we all make mistakes. If you do, admit it and learn from the mistake. Then go on and try to improve and grow. You'll be amazed at how much you'll learn.

Greeting Cards

Each of you should look not only to your own interests, but also to the interests of others.

—Philippians 2:4

Parenting is Heart WORK

Each of you should look not only to your own interests, but also to the interests of others.

—Philippians 2:4

Parenting is Heart WORK

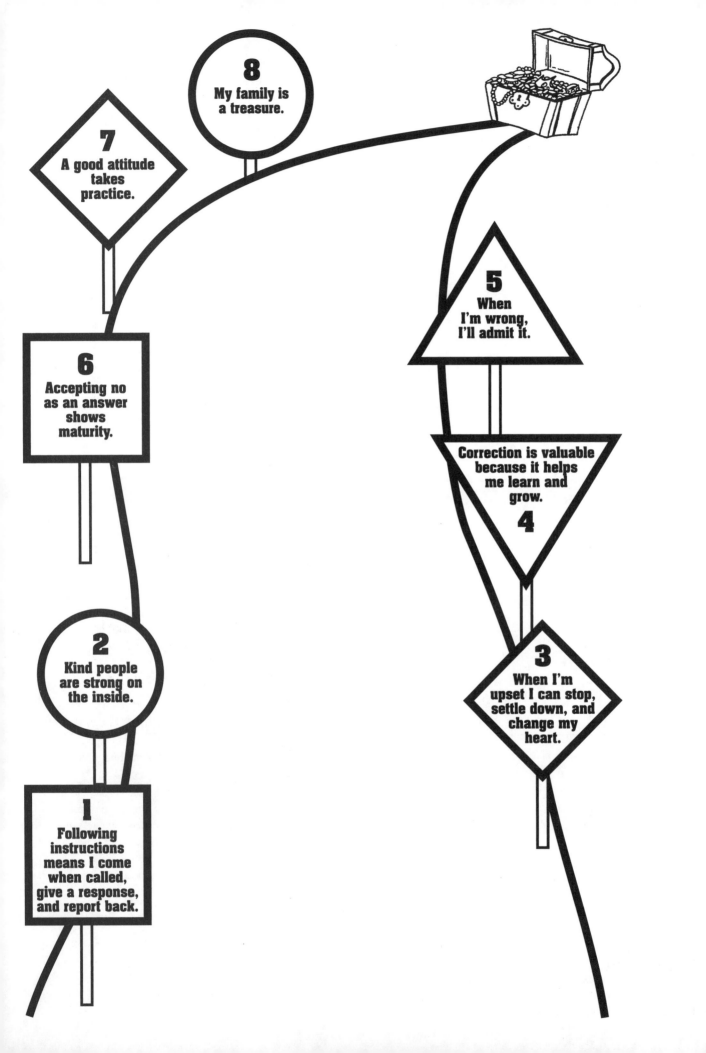

How to Play the Shooting Frog Game

Choose a destination you can call the lily pad at the other end of the house, quite a distance from the starting point. It should be some kind of large carpet or table providing plenty of room for landing. Distribute straws to each player. The first player slides the frog onto the launcher. By blowing into the straw the frog "jumps" or flies forward. The next player then gets a turn and so on until the frog makes it all the way to the lily pad. How many jumps did it take? Do it again and see if your family, working together, can reduce the number of jumps required to get to the lily pad.

How to Play the Shooting Frog Game

Choose a destination you can call the lily pad at the other end of the house, quite a distance from the starting point. It should be some kind of large carpet or table providing plenty of room for landing. Distribute straws to each player. The first player slides the frog onto the launcher. By blowing into the straw the frog "jumps" or flies forward. The next player then gets a turn and so on until the frog makes it all the way to the lily pad. How many jumps did it take? Do it again and see if your family, working together, can reduce the number of jumps required to get to the lily pad.

Session 8

Find Your Animal Partner

Find Your Animal Partner

76 Hopatcong Drive, Lawrenceville, NJ 08648-4136
(800) 771-8334 or (609) 771-8002
Email: parent@biblicalparenting.org
Web: biblicalparenting.org

Avoiding the Martha Mistake

Dear Parent,

Relationships take work. You know that but kids don't often realize what it takes to keep relationships open and close. In this lesson we used the story of Mary and Martha in the Bible to help kids see that Jesus affirmed Mary for listening instead of Martha who was more focused on her own list of things to do.

We used the Bible verse Philippians 2:4 "Each of you should look not only to your own interests, but also to the interests of others," to help kids think about others in family life and ways they might contribute to the strength of your family.

Theme: My family is a treasure.

You might ask your child about the invisible handwriting activity we did and how we crossed the room with pillows. Your child also made a frog game to take home and play with you and the family. It's our goal that your child might look for ways to strengthen family life by initiating fun, listening to others, and helping out.

You might try to reinforce the principle this week by telling your child what you appreciate about his or her contribution to family life. Be careful to not just focus on what you wish kids would do or what they aren't doing. Try to motivate your child with a positive vision of what family is.

The craft is a review of the eight principles children need to be successful in their families. You may want to use this craft to remind your child about key truths. Parenting is the hardest job in the world. If you'd like more help, maybe you'd like to sign up for free email parenting tips from the National Center for Biblical Parenting. You can visit the web site at www.biblicalparenting.org.

Blessings,

Scott Turansky   Joanne Miller
National Center for Biblical Parenting
www.biblicalparenting.org

Parenting is Heart WORK

Video Series

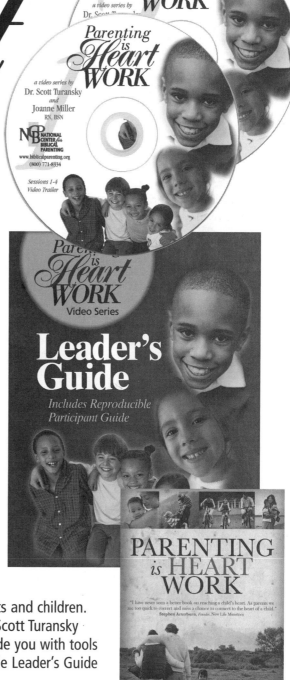

You'll love the movie! Use this eight-part video series in your church, small group, or even in your own family.

This video series complements the Treasure Hunters Children's Curriculum. As parents watch the videos they'll learn:

- A 5-step process for giving instructions that will build cooperation and responsibility in your kids

- Seven categories of consequences to fill up your "Toolbox"

- How to address thinking errors in children

- A plan for correction to help kids make lasting changes

- Plus many more practical ideas to use every day

The videos were filmed before a live audience of parents and children. Using drama, Bible stories, and lots of illustrations, Dr. Scott Turansky and Joanne Miller, RN, BSN will energize you and provide you with tools you need to strengthen your family. Use the reproducible Leader's Guide to give handouts to all participants.

To learn more give us a call or visit biblicalparenting.org

76 Hopatcong Drive
Lawrenceville, NJ 08648-4136
Phone: (800) 771-8334
Email: parent@biblicalparenting.org

Free i
EMAIL PARENTING Tips

Receive guidance and inspiration a couple of times a week in your inbox.

Free Parenting Tips

Get practical suggestions to help you relate better to your kids and help your kids change their hearts, not just their behavior.

The tips are gleaned from the live seminars, books, and articles of Dr. Scott Turansky and Joanne Miller, RN, BSN. Here's what parents are saying about these short words of encouragement.

"We have a three year old and an eight year old, and so many tips apply to both. It's exciting for me when God delivers a tip on something we're struggling with and I'm able to share it with my husband. It get's conversation started and good things happen."

—mom of two, Wichita, KS

"Just wanted to let you know what a blessing your parenting tips have been to me and the others I share them with. I make copies of them to pass around and also save them on file. They truly help me and other parents learn practical and biblical principles of parenting."

—children's pastor, San Diego, CA

"These tips are very helpful and actually seem to come at a time when I need them. I have three teenagers ages 16, 14, and 13, so I always need help with something."

—mom of three, Ewing, NJ

To receive Free Email Parenting Tips sign up online at www.biblicalparenting.org or fill out the form at the left and mail. Also available in Spanish. Visit www.padresefectivos.org.

Sign up for free email parenting tips now. (You can remove yourself from the list at any time.) Your email address will not be shared or sold to others.

Name

Address

City

State   Zip

Phone number with area code

Email address

NATIONAL CENTER for BIBLICAL Parenting

76 Hopatcong Drive
Lawrenceville, NJ 08648-4136
(800) 771-8334 or (609) 771-8002
Email: parent@biblicalparenting.org
Web: biblicalparenting.org